LIVING

IN

COLOR

By Jenny McDermid

ISBN: 1453656596
ISBN-13: 9781453656594

Jenny McDermid has counseled hundreds of women struggling with the aftermath of their abortion experiences. I have discovered, through written evaluations of her work and interviews with those who have met with her, that woman after woman has found Jenny a steadfast companion on the unique and isolating journey through post abortion grief.

Jenny is compassionate and insightful. In this book she shares her philosophy and model for helping women move from the deadness of post-abortion pain to a life of freedom and peace.

The woman who has yet to find a safe place to share her healing journey will find this book invaluable. And if she can complete the program within a facilitator-led support group, so much the better.

Women wounded by abortion no longer need to suffer alone in silence. This book will not only be instrumental for the next generation of post-abortion healing, but is an absolute must read for anyone who cares about post abortion grief.

Wendy Lowe
Executive Director
Calgary Pregnancy Care Centre

TABLE OF CONTENTS

INTRODUCTION

Deep healing after an abortion requires acknowledging and grieving the losses that have occurred. If you are willing to commit to it wholeheartedly, this *LIVING IN COLOR* program can guide you through the process and on to a healed and restored life.

The most effective way to complete this program is to find a confidential, facilitator-led *LIVING IN COLOR* support group in your area. Refer to www.pregcare.com for help in finding such a group.

Alternatively, you may set up weekly one-on-one meetings with a mentor, counselor, or pastor to support you as you complete the program. Making this healing journey in the company of such a person, or a support group, will offer comfort, accountability, and encouragement.

A *LIVING IN COLOR FACILITATOR GUIDE* is available for those leading groups. It would also be helpful for a mentor, counselor, or pastor working with a woman one-on-one. The guide is available through www.pregcare.com.

This program will take time, soul searching, and honesty. Your responses to questions must be authentic: it is pointless scribbling down answers just to fill the space provided. If you cannot answer a question right away, simply leave a blank, but do go back and try again after some time to reflect.

The majority of your answers will be recorded in this *LIVING IN COLOR* workbook. However, there are a number of exercises that require extra space for writing. A journal that lies flat when open, is big enough to invite your words, and has a pleasant color and quality of paper is ideal. Or a ring-binder and extra paper may suit you better. You will also need a highlighter for marking passages that capture your attention in the introductions to each exercise.

Journal writing over and above your workbook requirements can be helpful as a warm-up before starting a chapter, or for further processing of challenging areas. Suggestions for creating a sanctuary and journaling prompts are included in the appendices at the end of this workbook along with some other helpful resources.

Recovery and healing from abortion require digging into places you would rather not disturb. Please understand that uprooting pain and getting rid of it are necessary parts of the process; the path will become bleaker before it becomes brighter. However, consider how you are feeling right now—is this how you want to live forever? Now consider how you will feel having your recovery and healing behind you. In a couple of months you may hardly recognize yourself.

Once you have decided to confront the challenge, try to keep a vision of "living in color" before you as encouragement along the way.

CHAPTER ONE

GROUND ZERO

GROUND ZERO

Embarking on this journey has taken a tremendous amount of courage. It takes great determination to come out of hiding, to face yourself and others, to share your personal story, and to take ownership of the damage that your abortion decision has caused.

This introduction is called "Ground Zero" because that is what our lives tend to feel like, even if we pretend otherwise. Life was going along as usual when all of a sudden, out of the clear blue sky, came an experience of such destruction that all that remains is an aching, rubble-strewn void. But, just like the clearing and restoration of Ground Zero, we trust that you will find hope and healing as you work through this *Living in Color* program.

The only way to heal is to be willing to identify, confront, and experience the painful unresolved aspects and losses of the abortion experience and to dismantle the lies and unhealthy coping tactics we have adopted to survive.

Our goals are

To grieve our abortion losses
To restore faith and trust in ourselves
To bring health to broken relationships with God and others
To identify and control our triggers
To say "hello" and "goodbye" to our children
To find peace, closure, and new purpose

Program Topics

1. Ground Zero
2. No Man's Land
3. Curling Up
4. Volcanic Activity
5. Finding Wings
6. Hello There!
7. Goodbye for Now
8. Living In Color

Silence can be deafening to women struggling alone with the pain of their abortions. What we desperately need is someone to listen, someone who understands what we're going through, someone who won't condemn us or minimize what has happened.

T. Jackson

CONFRONTING THE CHALLENGE

Congratulations on taking the first steps of your journey to healing and recovery from the pain that follows an abortion decision.

Like many women before you, you may be bravely looking forward to facing this challenge one minute, and then feel like curling up in utter terror and despair the next. This feeling of being pulled back and forth may creep up on you throughout the program and needs to be ignored.

Try to be as strong as you can, but as gentle with yourself as you would be with a close friend who is going through a difficult time.

1. **Briefly describe a challenge you have faced. This could be a trip, a hike, or even a difficult work project.**

2. **Choose a word or two—brave, confident, excited, crazy, exhausted, triumphant, nervous, or depressed are good examples—to describe how you felt during each of these different stages:**

    • **The planning process**

    • **The first steps of the actual process**

    • **Halfway through**

    • **The end**

    • **As you looked back several months later**

3. **From these memories, what can you expect to encounter when facing a challenging experience?**

4. **How do you plan to encourage yourself when the going gets tough on this healing journey?**

5. Who will you ask to encourage you during this journey?

6. Have you tried to make a healing journey from post-abortion pain before? Did it help?

7. What are you committed to doing, or not doing, this time to make sure that you are successful?

Courage does not roar. Sometimes courage is the quiet voice at the end of the day saying, "I will try again tomorrow."

Maryanne Radmacher

ANATOMY OF CHANGE

There is a predictable pattern involved when making a decision to change:

- **Pre-contemplation**   Not yet thinking about changing your unsatisfactory condition

- **Contemplation**   Thinking about making a change

- **Determination**   Deciding to make a change and designing a plan

- **Action**   Taking the steps necessary to make the change happen

- **Maintenance**   Living your changed life intentionally and paying close attention to any influence that would seek to undermine your new status

1. **Which stage are you at today?**

2. **How does that make you feel?**

3. **Do you have any comments to yourself that you would like to record?**

You're braver than you believe, and stronger than you seem, and smarter than you think.
Christopher Robin to Winnie the Pooh

PARTICIPANT QUOTES

The following thoughts were shared by women who have completed their healing journeys:

It (the healing program) met me where I was: chaotic, depressed, self-blaming, shameful, guarded, somewhat defensive, and worked with me through relief, wonder, approachability, camaraderie, acceptance and sadness.

It (the healing program) was amazing ~ life-saving medicine, safe, accepting, encouraging. It was wonderful, it made me feel again.

The reality of symptoms (that I've been ashamed of) being discussed openly as reasonable reactions to abortion is new and refreshing.

I feel the program was absolutely fabulous. I was set free from guilt and pain. The homework was time-consuming and painful, but necessary. The connection within the group and the non judgmental feedback were very healing.

Sharing in the group with the other women was most helpful. I have always had problems relating to other women because of my abortions. Being accepted and loved by the other women was huge for me.

Shame and fear were my major feelings. I was unable to disclose my abortions. Secrets were hidden, buried. I was unable to admit that I had had the abortions, and unable to have healthy relationships with men or women.

With gentleness, firmness, and compassion, I was given encouragement to speak about my abortions, and I was given permission to own my abortions and begin to grieve those losses.

I feel incredibly grateful that this group was offered. I carried my abortion burdens alone for twenty-one years and felt that I could never tell anyone about them, let alone acknowledge my children and have a memorial service! I feel grateful, free, real. This program is awesome!

I now realize the impact my abortions have had on my life: I spent so much time and energy and emotion hiding my abortions that I was stuck, unable to grow and become the woman God wants me to be. I am amazed at how far I have come.

The kindness, understanding, and guidance extended to me have been lifesaving. A million thankyous would not be enough to express my gratitude. The program was the miracle I wondered if I would ever find. You helped me find my way back to God.

HEADS UP!

1. An abortion is an intense and painful personal experience and dealing with it is a challenging journey.

2. Find a trusted friend or family member who will offer extra support during this period of your life.

3. Process one abortion at a time.

4. This program is not difficult, but it can be intense. You may feel emotional and cry a lot. Grieving is helpful, as you are releasing bottled-up emotions that must be healed. Think of your tears as dissolving away the pain.

5. You may gradually remember things about your abortion experience that you have forgotten, or blocked out, because they were too painful to think about.

6. You may feel worse before you feel better. Reactions include feeling overwrought or depressed, or having vivid dreams—all normal responses.

7. Watch out for triggers. These are the experiences that connect you back to your abortion trauma, and they can cause distress, confusion, and unpredictable reactions. Record them on the next page as you identify them.

8. There are widely held ideas about grieving that are simply not true. Ignore any suggestions that you should keep your grief to yourself, or bury your feelings. Time does not heal in and of itself, and simply replacing your losses will never release you from pain. Grieving is a journey for which there are no shortcuts; the only way to heal is to take the steps required.

No-one can predict or prescribe healing for another. Each healing is as unique as the person going through it...Body, mind, and spirit are severely wounded by grief. All need healing. Each part of the human body and soul needs restoration and renewal. It takes time...
                                                                                Mary A. White

GETTING TO KNOW MY TRIGGERS

A trigger is something that connects you back to your abortion experience and causes un-predictable emotional reactions.

For example, you may have always disliked going to your dental appointments. But since your abortion, whenever you go to the dental clinic, your heart races, your hands become clammy, and panic threatens to overwhelm you.

There is a valid reason. The clinical odors, the receptionist behind her desk, or even sitting in the waiting room, may remind you of the abortion clinic and what happened there. A trig-ger is at work.

We will be working on identifying and managing your triggers later in the program.

For now, simply record any triggers as you identify them:

1.

2.

3

4.

5.

6.

7.

BALANCE

Emotional difficulties following abortion tend to affect many parts of our lives. We may feel, in the midst of our pain, that there is no hope of ever being healthy again, whether emotionally, relationally, mentally, physically, or spiritually. For this reason, a look at both our gains and our losses may help us regain a sense of balance.

Gains in our lives need to be celebrated. Losses need to be grieved. Although we will be addressing only losses related to your abortion in this program, this exercise should help you achieve some healthy perspective that all is not hopeless. You may also identify other areas that you can celebrate or grieve at a later date.

1. Complete the **TIMELINE DIAGRAM** on the next page, beginning at birth and ending with today.

2. Mark your major gains and your approximate age to the right of the line. Gains may include an award, graduation, friendship, marriage, rewarding job, baby's birth, or mastery of a skill, etc.

3. Now mark your major losses and age to the left of the line. Losses may include a significant break-up, divorce, the death of a loved one, abuse, loss of virginity, abortion, job loss, abandonment, bankruptcy, disability, depression, etc.

4. On your diagram, circle the gains that you have celebrated well, and the losses that you have grieved well. List them below.

        WELL-GRIEVED LOSSES: **WELL-CELEBRATED GAINS:**

5. What do the lists above tell you about how you have lived your life so far?

MY TIMELINE DIAGRAM

LOSSES   Today   GAINS

Birth

WHAT'S THE MATTER WITH ME?

You would not be on this journey unless you had a strong sense that all is not well in your world and suspected that your abortion may be, at least partly, to blame. A small percentage of women feel peaceful about their decision to have an abortion, experience relief once it is done, and are able to live without regret. You may have hoped to be one of these.

However, the unfortunate reality is that the majority of women experience significant emotional turmoil following their abortion that may include some, or many, of the following reactions.

1. **Please highlight those that apply to you:**

    - **Sadness and/or feelings of loss**
    - **Numbness and a tendency to avoid thinking about the abortion**
    - **Increase in dangerous or unhealthy activities (alcohol/drug abuse, eating disorders, cutting, casual and indifferent sex, and other risk-taking behaviors)**
    - **Depression for more than two weeks that is stronger than "the blues"**
    - **Anxiety, panic attacks, or an increase in phobias**
    - **Suicidal or self-harming thoughts or attempts**
    - **Obsessive thoughts about the abortion procedure, or a tendency to block recall and details of the experience**
    - **Nightmares and/or difficulty sleeping**
    - **Flashbacks to the abortion experience**
    - **Tendency to startle easily or to feel overly alert**
    - **Obsessive control over people, procedures, or things**
    - **Difficulty making decisions**
    - **Loss of interest in usual significant activities**
    - **Inability to perform normal self-care activities**
    - **Loss of interest in dreams and goals**
    - **Inability to function normally at school or work**
    - **Problems caring for home, children, or husband/partner**
    - **Relationship difficulties with partner or other relationships**
    - **Smothering or distancing oneself from one's children**
    - **Problems with sex and physical intimacy**
    - **Avoidance of pregnant women, babies, or children**
    - **Distress when exposed to abortion or sanctity of life topics on TV, in magazines, or in conversation**
    - **Feelings of guilt and shame**
    - **Inappropriate anger**
    - **Fear surrounding future fertility**
    - **Obsession with excelling at school or work**

- **A desire to become pregnant to "replace" the baby that was lost**
- **Painful reactions on anniversary of abortion or due date**

Abortion is a traumatic event, and many women continue to struggle with the fallout for months or years. If you have highlighted several of the above symptoms, you are probably suffering from that fallout. It does have a name: post-abortion stress (PAS).

Post-abortion stress is sometimes incorrectly referred to as a "syndrome." We will simply refer to the fallout from abortion as "post-abortion stress" or "PAS." There are similarities between PAS and PTSD (post-traumatic stress disorder), a reaction to traumatic events such as war, disaster, accident, or assault.

Please be assured that recovery is possible. Your journey of healing will require some work, but anything worth achieving usually does.

2. **Use this space to record any thoughts or feelings you are having as you reflect on the reactions that you have highlighted. In particular, note those that you find surprising— reactions that you would not have connected to your abortion experience.**

The first step in dealing with trauma is to recognize its impact. A traumatic event has many possible impacts. It can impact your feelings, thoughts, relationships, behaviors, attitudes, dreams and hopes. However, it can also be a way to find a new direction and purpose in life.
Mary Beth Williams & Soili Poijula

MY ABORTION WOUND

Visualizing your abortion wound is one way of getting in touch with its reality and effect on your life. It is also helpful for keeping track of your healing progress. By describing your wound at the beginning, you create a starting point for later reference.

Everyone will have a different description of her abortion wound. The following examples may be helpful:

- *Some years after my abortion, I realized that I felt like something made of glass that had been dropped onto concrete and had shattered into a mass of ugly, splintered shards. I sensed that if anyone came near enough to touch me, or to help me, they would be cut by the razor-sharp edges and I would cause them to be wounded too.*

- *My wound seemed like a meadow that was once a lush and lovely place, full of beautiful flowers. But then it had been horribly polluted and everything had died. There was now only blackened, bare earth with bits and pieces of dead vegetation ~ nothing could ever grow there again.*

Please use the space below to draw, or describe in words, the emotional wound from your abortion experience. If you prefer, you can create a collage instead.

CHOOSE YOUR BELIEFS CAREFULLY

1. **Read this excerpt several times, highlighting anything that seems to jump out at you.**

    Our beliefs have a direct and profound effect on how we feel and act. For example, if you believe that you can't live without the person you have lost, or that you will never be happy again, that belief will control your actions, thoughts, and feelings. It will keep you depressed and bogged down in self-pity and will block your recovery.

    We may not always live what we profess, but we always live consistently with what we believe.

    Our beliefs are like a built-in automatic pilot...If we believe we are unlovable, we will act in an unlovable manner. If we believe we are a failure, we will set ourselves up to fail. If we believe we are basically bad, we will act badly. Conversely, if we believe we are lovable, we will act in a loving manner. Life is a series of belief choices, and we are in a sense the sum total of all those choices. We believe what we choose to believe, what we want to believe.

    If we choose to believe, therefore, that we can't get over our loss, we handicap our recovery. If we believe we can overcome it, we assist it. The choice is ours. It's in our hands. So choose your beliefs carefully.[1]

    Dick Innes

2. **What positive thing have you believed about yourself that turned out to be true?**

3. **What negative thing have you believed about yourself that turned out to be true?**

[1] Dick Innes *How to Mend a Broken Heart* (Grand Rapids, MI: Fleming H Revell 1994) pgs 19-20.

4.   **State three things that you believe about post-abortion recovery that are likely to assist your recovery:**

   •   **Post-abortion recovery is…**

   •   **Post-abortion recovery is…**

   •   **Post-abortion recovery is…**

5.   **Do you agree that your beliefs affect your life? Why?**

6.   **Find a picture of a person or scene that depicts the healthy emotional state you hope to achieve by the end of this program.**

It doesn't cost me extra to believe I can beat this. But it costs me everything to believe I can't.
Jeth Weinrich ~ former crack addict

FEELINGS INVENTORY

AFFECTIONATE: appealing, cherishing, close, loving, nurturing, passionate, seductive, sexy, tender, warm.

AFRAID: alarmed, anxious, appalled, apprehensive, awed, cautious, concerned, cowardly, dependent, dismayed, doubtful, exposed, fearful, fidgety, frightened, gutless, hesitant, horrified, hysterical, impatient, insecure, nervous, panicky, petrified, powerless, pressured, scared, shaky, shocked, suspicious, terrified, threatened, timid, tragic, worried.

ANGRY: aggressive, annoyed, awkward, belligerent, bewildered, bitter, boiling, cross, enraged, frustrated, fuming, furious, grumpy, indignant, inflamed, infuriated, irate, irritated, offended, provoked, resentful, scary, stubborn, sulky, sullen, vengeful, violent, wrathful.

DOUBTFUL: confused, defeated, distrustful, dubious, evasive, helpless, hesitant, indecisive, perplexed, pessimistic, powerless, questioning, skeptical, suspicious, unbelieving, uncertain, wavering.

EAGER: anxious, avid, enthusiastic, excited, intent, interested, keen, zealous.

FEARLESS: ambitious, bold, brave, confident, courageous, daring, determined, encouraged, hardy, heroic, impulsive, independent, loyal, proud, reassured, secure, settled, unwavering.

HAPPY: buoyant, brisk, calm, carefree, cheerful, comfortable, contented, ecstatic, elated, enthusiastic, excited, exhilarated, festive, generous, glad, grateful, hilarious, inspired, jolly, joyful, lighthearted, optimistic, peaceful, playful, pleased, relaxed, restful, satisfied, serene, sparkling, spirited, surprised, thrilled, vivacious.

HURT: aching, afflicted, agonized, cold, crushed, cut off, despairing, distressed, dumped, gutted, heartbroken, injured, isolated, lonely, lost, offended, pained, pathetic, shattered, suffering, tortured, undone, worried.

INTERESTED: absorbed, concerned, curious, engaged, engrossed, excited, fascinated, intrigued.

MISCELLANEOUS: ashamed, blessed, bored, cruel, distant, envious, faithful, humble, jealous, preoccupied, privileged, proud, torn, trusting, wishy-washy.

PHYSICAL: alive, breathless, empty, feisty, hollow, immobilized, nauseated, paralyzed, repelled, sluggish, stressed, stretched, strong, sweaty, taut, tense, tired, uptight, weak, weary.

SAD: blah, blue, choked up, compassionate, concerned, disappointed, discouraged, dismal, dreadful, dreary, dull, embarrassed, flat, gloomy, heavy-hearted, ill at ease, in the dumps, low, melancholic, messed up, moody, mournful, out of sorts, quiet, somber, sorrowful, sulky, sullen, sympathetic, shameful, unhappy, useless, worthless.

CHAPTER TWO

NO MAN'S LAND

NO MAN'S LAND

"No Man's Land" is the name given to an area between the borders of two neighboring countries. Typically desolate and bleak, the area belongs to neither. A person stuck in No Man's Land may have no documents allowing entry to either country, or she may have left one country but have yet to enter the other.

When we experience abortion, we emotionally leave our old country, where life carries on as we once knew it. The new country where we can experience a healing journey is beyond the next border.

Living in denial is the equivalent of sitting down in the middle of No Man's Land and refusing to move. There is no going back to life as it was before, and yet we feel unable to face the new country either. So there we stay, coping as best we can but growing ever conscious of the fact that all is not well.

In this chapter we will dismantle the denial, avoidance, and secrecy surrounding our abortion experiences. This process will involve telling our stories. Please don't panic! You will be helped enormously by the crafting and telling of your story in a safe place with safe people who care about you.

Denial feelings were like a force field. As long as I didn't touch them, I was okay.

Jason

RELIEF

We are all familiar with what relief feels like—that moment when we can say, "Whew!" after a situation is resolved. Perhaps physical pain is relieved, a threat is removed, or enormous stress over an agonizing decision is behind us.

Abortion promises to relieve the stress of bringing a child into the world before we are ready, and offers to rescue us from enormous responsibilities and changes to our lives. However, although it delivers on that promise, there is a heavy price to pay.

Your decision to abort may have been a hasty one involving little thought, but for many it involves a certain amount of time and a great deal of stress. The period of decision-making often involves communication landmines, moral dilemmas, relationship stress, and the conflict of see-sawing emotions.

Consequently, having the abortion procedure behind us can produce immense feelings of relief. At least the decision is made: there's no turning back, no more nausea, no more pressure-packed conversations and sleepless nights.

1.   **Did any of the following situations bring you relief? Describe whether it was "some" relief, or "a lot," and record any memorable feelings you have from each situation:**

   a)   **When you shared your pregnancy with a trusted person?**

   b)   **When the father of your baby promised to be there for you, and you imagined there might be a "happy ever after" together?**

   c)   **When you finally made your decision?**

d)   When you made your abortion appointment?

e)   When you were in recovery after the procedure?

f)   When you came home after the procedure?

g)   The next day?

h)   A few weeks later?

2.   How long would you estimate the feeling of relief after your abortion lasted?

DENIAL

Unfortunately, relief is seldom a feeling that lasts. The sad reality is that abortion simply trades one set of stressors for another as the reality of what has taken place begins to sink in. This new scenario can be so distressing that it can lead to a condition called "denial." The word "denial" refers to a refusal to acknowledge a difficult truth or emotion, or to admit it into consciousness. It is used as an emotional defense strategy, or shield.

In fact, denial is a God-given gift to protect you from emotional pain that is too harsh to cope with, but only for a short period of time. If you remain in denial for too long, you are in danger of developing a habit of self-deception and avoidance that will cause even more emotional distress in the long run.

1. **Think back to your abortion experience and try to describe any denial you used at these different stages:**

   a) **In my relationship I denied...**

   b) **When my period was late, I denied...**

   c) **When I discovered I was pregnant, I denied...**

   d) **While making the decision to abort, I denied...**

e) At the clinic/hospital I denied...

f) Immediately after the procedure, I denied...

g) Six months later I denied...

h) Today I am denying...

2. A common acronym for denial is FINE:

Feelings
Inside
Never
Expressed

Now that you have delved into your own use of denial, write a few sentences describing what you have learned.

AVOIDANCE

Avoidance is a denial technique whereby we refuse to engage with difficult thoughts, emotions, or memories. When reminders come up, we simply direct our minds to veer away from engaging with them.

Avoidance can protect us from unwelcome trigger reactions, so it is not uncommon to develop a habit of avoiding people, places, or activities that remind us of the abortion. However, avoidance doesn't solve anything in the long run. Rather, it causes us to feel anxious, fearful, irritable, and powerless. Avoidance is a *defensive* tactic. What is needed is an *offensive* tactic: a healing journey that leads instead to wholeness, freedom, and peace.

1. **Highlight any of the following examples that seem familiar. Give details beneath those that apply to you.**

    I have avoided:

    a) **The father of my child and any reminders of him**

    b) **Places or activities I enjoyed at the time of my abortion**

    c) **Memories associated with my abortion**

    d) **Sexual intimacy**

    e) **Friends I enjoyed at the time of my abortion**

    f) **Family members who may accidentally find out**

g)   Sanctity of life or abortion topics in the media or discussions

h)   The doctor who referred me for the abortion

i)   The counselor who gave me advice before the abortion

j)   Hospitals, medical or dental clinics

k)   Vacuum cleaners

l)   Gynecological exams

m)   Pregnant women, babies, or baby showers

n)   Other

2.   Which three areas of avoidance have affected your quality of life the most?

MY SAFE PLACE

At times during your healing work, you may find yourself becoming extremely agitated or upset as you recall painful experiences. To cope with these emotions, it is helpful to visualize a "safe place," one that offers a sense of protection and security.

For ideas, think back to a time in your life when you felt, or imagined being, completely safe. Perhaps a cabin in the woods comes to mind: solid log walls, the smell of wood smoke from a crackling fire, rain drumming on the roof, a comfy sofa with a well-loved quilt to snuggle under, and a cup of hot chocolate.

Your safe place may be real—a childhood hideout, a cozy den, or the deserted beach you explored on a memorable summer vacation. Or it may be a place you long to be: a field of flowers, a castle with a moat and drawbridge, a small island in a calm sea. Whatever you choose, try to capture what it is about how this place looks, smells, sounds, or feels that makes it safe for you.

1. **Name your safe place.**

2. **Describe your safe place in words, a drawing, or a collage.**

3. **What is it about this place that makes you feel safe?**

BREAKING OUT OF DENIAL

Overcoming denial involves the careful dismantling of the coping strategies we have used to survive, and then a revisiting of the abortion in order to find closure. The crafting and telling of your story, later in this chapter, will help you with these steps. In the meantime, here's a handy acronym for breaking out of denial: **RATS!**

> **R**emembering
> **A**ccepting
> **T**aking ownership
> **S**houldering responsibility

1. **Consider the following examples of denial at the three stages of the abortion experience, and highlight any that seem familiar:**

Pre-abortion

- Denial of the pregnancy itself by saying, "I can't be pregnant!"

- Denial of responsibility by saying, "I had no choice!"

- Denial of decisions made by saying, "He forced me to do it!"

Abortion

- Denial of what it felt like physically or emotionally

- Denial of reality by thinking, "I can't handle these feelings, so I won't think about, express, or process them. I'll veer away from anything that reminds me of the abortion procedure."

Post-abortion

- Denial of certain aspects of the abortion

- Denial of all memories of the abortion

- Denial of the relationship between the abortion and self-defeating or self-destructive behaviors

2. **Now, complete the following statements as realistically as you can:**

- **Abortion is** *an act of desperation* (for example).

- **Abortion is...**

- **Abortion is...**

- **Abortion is...**

USES OF MEMORY

1. **Read this excerpt several times, highlighting the parts that grab your attention.**

I am inclined to believe that God's chief purpose in giving us memory is to enable us to go back in time so that if we didn't play those roles right the first time round, we can still have another go at it now.

We cannot undo our old mistakes or their consequences any more than we can erase old wounds that we have both suffered and inflicted, but through the power that memory gives us of thinking, feeling, imagining our way back through time we can at long last finally finish with the past in the sense of removing its power to hurt us and other people and to stunt our growth as human beings.

The sad things that happened long ago will always remain part of who we are just as the glad and gracious things will too, but instead of being a burden of guilt, recrimination, and regret that make us constantly stumble as we go, even the saddest things can become, once we have made peace with them, a source of wisdom and strength for the journey that still lies ahead.

It is through memory that we are able to reclaim much of our lives that we have long since written off by finding that in everything that has happened to us over the years God was offering us possibilities of new life and healing which, though we may have missed them at the time, we can still choose and be brought to life by and healed by all these years later.[2]

Frederick Buechner

2. **Now respond to the message you have received.**

---

2   Frederick Buechner *Telling Secrets* (New York: HarperCollins Publishers 1991)

WHO WAS I?

The trauma of abortion tends to divide our lives into "before" and "after," the person you were before being, typically, quite different from the one you became afterwards.

1. **Try to recall the kind of person you were before your abortion experience:**

    a)   **What kind of home life did you have growing up? Were you close to your parents and siblings?**

    b)   **What kind of student were you? Were you at school or working when you discovered that you were pregnant?**

    c)   **What kind of friendships did you have?**

    d)   **Were you passionate about certain hobbies or sports?**

    e)   **Were you happy, sad, shy, funny, confident, or introverted?**

    f)   **What were your greatest strengths? What were your most significant weaknesses?**

g)   **What role did God or faith play in your life?**

h)   **What was your dating or marriage history like?**

i)   **Did you have a definite opinion about abortion before your pregnancy occurred? What was it?**

2.   **Describe the kind of person you were, before you had your abortion, from the point of view of someone who knew you well.**

THE RELATIONSHIP

The relationship that led up to your abortion may have been anything from a one-night stand to an established marriage. You may have thought yourself deeply in love, or you may have felt ambivalent about your situation. Whatever the case, your relationship resulted in a pregnancy and needs to be examined before you progress further. Refer to the FEELINGS INVENTORY in the first chapter for suitable words, if necessary.

1.   **Allow yourself to think back to the relationship that resulted in your abortion.**

   a)   **What was his first name, how old were you both at the time, and how did you meet?**

   b)   **What were you doing at the time? Were you at school, working, raising a family, or on vacation?**

   c)   **Was the relationship a committed one? Were you calling him your "boyfriend," "partner," "live-in," or "husband"?**

   d)   **Did you already have other children? Did he?**

   e)   **How long had the relationship existed before the pregnancy occurred? Did you feel secure within the relationship, sure of his emotional commitment to you?**

   f)   **Were you together when you took the pregnancy test? If not, how did you break the news?**

g)   What was his reaction to finding out that you were pregnant?

h)   What did you wish that he had said or done?

i)   What were your gut-level responses to his reaction?

j)   What did you learn about him in those moments?

k)   Did your feelings towards him change as a result of his reaction?

l)   Are you still together? If not, how long did the relationship last after the abortion?

2.   How did you react as you answered these questions? Did you experience any intense feelings of sadness, hurt, betrayal, or anger? Did any of these memories make you cry?

3.   Do you feel as though you have covered the relationship well, genuinely allowing yourself to remember, feel, and respond? If not, please add further details about your relationship below.

THE DECISION

For many of us, the longing to go back and reconsider our decisions is a haunting and poignant companion. If only we had had more time, courage, information, support, or confidence in the relationship. Perhaps overwhelming nausea, or a health crisis for mother or baby played a role. But whether we wrestled with the decision for several months or made it in a heartbeat, the outcome was the same.

1. **By using the power of memory, you can revisit your decision and try to make sense of what took place.**

   a) **What were the major issues at stake as you were deciding? Were they relational, financial, physical, social, or moral? What role did school or career play? Divide the pie accordingly.**

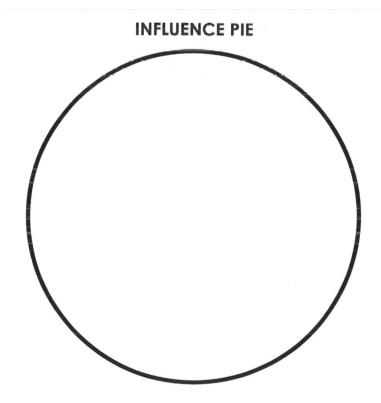

INFLUENCE PIE

   b) **What emotions affected your thinking? Were you influenced by panic, pride, desperation, or helplessness? Refer to the FEELINGS INVENTORY in the first chapter, for further ideas if necessary.**

c)   Did you seek counseling or other professional advice? Alone, or with your partner? Did it help?

d)   Did you involve family or friends in your decision-making? How did they influence your choice?

e)   Did you feel that you were rushed, or pressured, in any way? If so, by whom?

f)   Did either you or your partner waver back and forth about your decision?

g)   How long did it take your partner to decide on abortion? How long did it take you? How did you come to a unanimous decision?

h)   How many days, weeks, or months passed between discovering you were pregnant and the abortion procedure?

2.   Write a short letter to yourself, summarizing your understanding of the pressures that caused you to make the decision you made. Close with three things you would have changed.

Dear _____,

THE ABORTION

Don't be surprised if you simply can't remember certain details of your abortion experience. It is common to repress memories that are too difficult to bear.

1. **Recall what you can, and fill in as much detail as possible.**

    a) **How did you feel when you woke up on the day of your abortion? Do you remember the date or approximate time of year?**

    b) **What was the weather like? What did you wear?**

    c) **Did you go to a hospital or to a clinic? Who took you, and did they wait and bring you home too?**

    d) **What was the building like? Did the receptionist treat you kindly? When did you pay for the procedure?**

    e) **Did you receive any counseling or explanations about the procedure?**

    f) **Describe the waiting room. How did you feel as you waited?**

g)   What do you remember about the operating room? Were you frightened? Did you feel like changing your mind?

h)   How did the nurses treat you? The doctor?

i)   Were you awake, sedated, or anaesthetized? Do you have any memories of the procedure? Did any odors or sounds stand out?

j)   Do you remember feeling any pain?

k)   How did you feel when you woke up? Did you cry?

l)   What was the recovery room like? What happened there?

2.   Describe how you got home and what you did for the rest of the day. Include details of any support you received, or wished you had received, and how you responded to it.

TELL YOUR STORY

Telling your story is a powerful way of confronting the reality of what has happened. Writing it down first, in narrative form, helps you to remember who was involved, what happened, and the emotions that accompanied the experience. The process might seem intimidating—at least until you realize that you have already done most of the work by recording who you were, the relationship you were in, the decision-making process surrounding the abortion, and details of the abortion itself.

The true power of your story will be felt when you read it aloud in a safe environment, especially among those who have shared your experience. As with any trauma, processing the experience and then putting it into words will help heal the damage. And the more you are willing to speak the truth, the more potent your storytelling will be. In fact, one of the most powerful factors in preventing long-term post-traumatic stress is the ability to repeatedly talk about the trauma. Your story needs to be told again and again, as words solidify the experience and give you a sense of control.

The prospect of telling your story for the first time may seem extremely threatening. Each time you speak, however, your feelings of fear and vulnerability will lessen. Telling your story is like a slow detoxification process: the more you speak of your memories, the less power they will have to bring you pain.

As you review the situation surrounding your abortion, its significance in your life, and the grief you feel over the loss, you will be able to put your abortion into perspective and integrate it into your life's story. You will begin to understand that abortion does not need to define you: it is merely one small section of the huge jigsaw that makes up your life.

Telling your story will draw you out of No Man's Land and position you to continue your healing journey.

Write your story. You will have up to ten minutes to tell your story, so time yourself as you practice reading it aloud, slowly and clearly. Practicing will also help calm your nerves, and every reading will further your healing process.

I never wrote down these events before. Recollecting them was not pleasant but was, perhaps, therapeutic. It is good to shadow box with your memories. And for urging me to write, I thank you.

Tommy Dick

MAKEOVER MADNESS

Post-abortive women who have finally gathered the courage to take a stand and confront the dysfunctional situations in their lives often share some common reactions.

As they make headway with their recovery, they start to realize that they are, in fact, competent and deserving women. And, before long, they begin to realize that they may have been putting up with a lot of disrespect and ill-treatment from those around them.

Once these women have given themselves permission to identify the emotions they have been suppressing, they are often tempted to look around and see that all sorts of situations in their lives, besides their post-abortion pain, need an overhaul. They might lament that their husbands put them down, their kids treat them like a doormat, or their mother-in-law's idiosyncrasies have frayed their last nerve. Or perhaps their renovation frenzy turns inwards: they want to stop drinking, shed pounds, run a marathon, or become a domestic goddess. Makeover madness has set in!

However, taking on too many different issues at once is a recipe for disaster. What is needed is a steady focus on one goal at a time. Once the post-abortion healing journey has been made, the next most urgent goal can be addressed. And then the next...and so on. How do you eat an elephant? One bite at a time!

Make a list of issues you wish to tackle *after* you have completed your post-abortion healing:

1.

2.

3.

4.

5.

6.

7.

CHAPTER THREE

CURLING UP

CURLING UP

When we are suffering from the pain of guilt, shame, remorse, and sadness, we often withdraw into ourselves. Although this instinct is self-protective, it often inhibits healing. Healing is most often found in the safety of a nurturing community; unfortunately, however, the very people who could offer support and help are often the ones we cannot face.

"Curling up" comes at a cost. It is difficult to make progress when we are isolated with our chaotic emotions. If we cannot create order by talking about our problems, our emotions can become overwhelming—and gradually toxic.

Imagine a substitute teacher arriving in a classroom full of unruly children whose names she does not know. As she tries to get their attention and establish order, she finds that she is powerless. Chaos reigns. However, once she is armed with their names, she is empowered. Now she can call upon them one by one and gain control over the situation.

Taming our emotions is a similar exercise. When we feel overwhelmed, it is too easy to give in to despair and hopelessness. However, when we take the time to sort out those toxic emotions, identify them by name, and learn how to deal with them one by one, we are able to gain control and make progress with our healing.

Don't be dismayed by the various topics included in this chapter. Instead, be encouraged that you are in the process of naming and taming the fallout from your trauma in a safe and caring community.

Hope is like a bird that senses the dawn and carefully starts to sing while it is still dark.
Unknown

ISOLATION

1. **Read this excerpt several times, highlighting the parts that resonate with you.**

    Peace and healing come in the context of relationships. Mental anguish is an invisible wound that often goes unnoticed by others. As a result many women suffer alone and their healing is delayed. When you are healing, it is critical that you risk in relationships. Fight the inner voice that says, "don't talk about it; don't bother them with the details," and reach out to safe people. As you allow safe people to help you bear your burden by authentically sharing your thoughts and feelings, your healing will be accelerated. The opposite is also true. Isolation can retard growth and healing.

    It's natural to pull back from everyone and everything when we've suffered a wound, much as we would yank our finger away from a flame to protect ourselves from more burns. But if we remain recoiled and detached ~ closing God and others out of our suffering ~ we will derail our own healing.[3]

    Dr Steve Stephens and Pam Vredevelt

2. **Highlight any of the following ways in which you have isolated yourself since your abortion. Add a note if you understand the reason behind your behavior.**
    *   **I have withdrawn from my family**
    *   **I have isolated myself from school or work colleagues**
    *   **I have stopped caring about my school or career goals**
    *   **I have distanced myself from my dating or marriage partner**
    *   **I have stopped doing things that used to bring me pleasure**
    *   **I have stopped caring about how I look and how I dress**
    *   **I have stopped having regular health or dental check-ups**
    *   **I have isolated myself from involvement with babies or children**
    *   **I have distanced myself from my own children**
    *   **I have stopped attending church services or related activities**
    *   **I have distanced myself from God**
    *   **Other**

3. **What price are you paying to protect or punish yourself through isolation?**

---

3   Dr Steve Stephens and Pam Vredevelt *The Wounded Woman* (Sisters: Multnomah Publishers Inc 2006) pg 35.

THE GREY ZONE

Abortion is secret, shameful, traumatic, and sad. No matter who has been involved with the abortion decision, it is the woman who typically bears the burden of responsibility and the torment alone.

When a child is lost under other circumstances, the mother is often surrounded by supportive people. Those close to her expect her to be distraught and bereft; consequently, they assist her as she grieves. But acknowledging the loss of a child due to abortion seems somehow inappropriate and surreal.

Left alone, and refusing or unable to grieve her significant loss, a woman may enter the "Grey Zone." This is the name given to the numb, colorless, hopeless condition that is experienced by those who live with unresolved grief.

Stuck in the "Grey Zone," many women adopt a life of pretense, putting on a mask, pretending that all is well, and soldiering on as best they can. However, the very nature of a mask is that it separates a woman from authentic living and healthy relationships. This barrier may lead to loneliness, despair, depression, addiction, and worse.

1.   **Can you identify times that you have experienced life in the "Grey Zone"? Describe what that feels like.**

2.   **Have you been trying to pretend that life is just fine when deep down you know that it is not? Try to describe how this pretense has affected your life and relationships.**

I was afraid to think about my abortion. I couldn't allow myself to think of my abortion as a loss. For years I did not even know what was wrong with me. I never identified the source of my anger and pain. I just know I was hurting inside...real bad. I cut myself off from my feelings. I was always numb.
From "Forbidden Grief" by Theresa Burke

GUILT & SHAME

After an abortion, our sense of guilt and shame is usually profound: there may appear to be no escape from self-loathing and despair. A common side effect is a growing sense of unworthiness or inferiority that, in turn, may lead us to sabotage our opportunities for happiness and success. However, guilt and shame are very different from one another. Understanding them will help us heal.

Guilt is a message that tells us we have offended our personal moral or ethical boundaries. Our conscience is writhing because *we have done something wrong*. Guilt can be healthy, prompting us to recognize our mistake, seek forgiveness, and find peace.

Shame is a message that tells us that *there is something wrong with us*. It is ultimately destructive, as it labels us worthless, and therefore condemns and isolates us. Guilt inspires us to face the truth, and then seek forgiveness and restoration. Shame, on the other hand, is based on a lie, a lie that can unleash a cascade of negative forces.

1. **Do you feel guilty about your abortion? If so, list reasons why:**

2. **Has your guilt caused you to take action, either positive or negative? Explain.**

3. **Many women find that the Bible can speak into their lives, especially on their healing journeys. Read the verses that follow. Then describe what God wants you to do about your guilt and what you can expect to happen.**

   Finally, I confessed all my sins to you and stopped trying to hide my guilt. I said to myself, "I will confess my rebellion to the Lord." And you forgave me! All my guilt is gone.

   Psalm 32:5

   "Come, let's talk this over," says the Lord. "Though your sins are like scarlet, they shall be as white as snow; though they are red as crimson, they shall be like wool."

   Isaiah 1:18

4. Do you struggle with believing the promises in these verses? Can you explain why?

5. Here are some common lies we tell ourselves regarding abortion. Respond to each with a truth statement as in the example below:

LIE	TRUTH
• I didn't have a choice	*I could have said "no" to abortion*
• It was just a clump of cells	
• Abortion is legal so it must be okay	
• My abortion was no big deal	
• It's my body—I can do what I like with it	
• The baby would have interfered with my life	
• I'm doing just fine	
• I'm a terrible person	
• I'll never get over this	
• It was the best decision I could have made	

6. Highlight any of the following major feelings associated with shame that you can identify with:

    • Worthlessness

    • Inadequacy or inferiority

    • Fear of intimacy

    • Lack of trust

    • Oppressive thoughts and feelings

    • Defensiveness

7. **Read these verses and record what is needed to conquer shame.**

Those who look to him for help will be radiant with joy; no shadow of shame will darken their faces.

Psalm 34:5

Those who trust in me will never be put to shame.

Isaiah 9:23b

Fear not; you will no longer live in shame. Don't be afraid; there is no more disgrace for you.

Isaiah 54:4

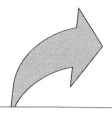

GOD

God forgives me
and
draws me back into
the light and
into
intimacy with him

GUILT CYCLE

God uses
GUILT
to convict me of
**SOMETHING I'VE
DONE WRONG**

This causes me to…
**CONFESS
REPENT
&
ASK FOR
FORGIVENESS**

This causes me to
descend into…
**CONDEMNATION
ISOLATION
&
DESPAIR**

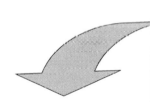

Hopelessness
forces me
downwards
and
deeper into
darkness

SHAME CYCLE

Darkness causes
SHAME
to convince me that
there is
**SOMETHING
WRONG WITH ME**

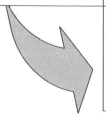

DARKNESS

FEAR & ANXIETY

Fear is a sense of danger or fright that has a particular focus. Anxiety, on the other hand, is a stifling sense of tension and dread whose source cannot be easily pinpointed. Fear is easier to identify than anxiety because it is triggered by something concrete. Anxiety feels more like a smothering fog of unease. Unlike worries, which everyone experiences from time to time, fear and anxiety can interfere with everyday living or last for a long time.

1. **After an abortion, numerous fears may surface.**

   a) **Please highlight any of the following that apply to you:**

      • **Medical clinics/hospitals**

      • **Doctors/nurses**

      • **Gynecological examinations**

      • **Waiting rooms**

      • **Anesthetics**

      • **Medical procedures**

      • **Sounds of abortion equipment**

      • **Others finding out about the abortion**

      • **Loss of control**

      • **God's punishment**

      • **Future infertility**

      • **Other?**

   b) **A phobia is an extreme fear that involves the avoidance, at all cost, of some object, person, or situation. Note any fears that have developed into a phobia for you.**

2. **Anxiety becomes a problem when it takes over your life.**

   a) **Please highlight any of the following that apply to you:**

      • **Expecting the worst**

      • **Excessive worry about health, money, or family**

      • **Difficulty maintaining relationships**

- Difficulty making decisions
- Trouble concentrating or remembering
- Difficulty keeping a job
- Inability to relax
- Severe muscle tension in neck, back, and shoulders
- Trembling, twitching, sweating
- Headaches, tiredness, irritability
- Difficulty sleeping

b) Anguish is intense anxiety that can lead to significant responses. Highlight any of the following symptoms that you have experienced. Describe what took place.

• Panic Attacks	Anxiety becomes unbearable, your heart pounds, and you become dizzy, shaky, and breathless.
• Obsessive Thoughts	These may repeat for days, months, or years and may, or may not, be directly linked to the abortion experience.
• Obsessive Behaviors	You become inflexible, perfectionistic or obsessive about things or people. Behaviors might include constant hand washing, checking that doors are locked, plucking hair, picking at skin, setting impossible standards for yourself or others, etc.

3. Release from fear and anxiety comes when you confront the pain and stress that are at the root of your turmoil. In the space below, find or draw a picture of a person carrying a heavy burden. Think of the physical cost of that effort, and then imagine the relief that comes when the weight is removed.

Then Jesus said, "Come to me, all of you who are weary and carry heavy burdens, and I will give you rest."

Matthew 11:28

DEPRESSION

Most people feel down from time to time. Usually these feelings are short-lived, and we feel like ourselves again once the situation improves. However, more serious feelings of depression are common among women suffering from post-abortion stress.

The pain of constantly reliving the experience or reacting to reminders of the event can lead to depression. Depression enables us to withdraw from our painful reality. However, over time this withdrawal can have a profound effect on our ability to function normally. If left untreated for long periods, depression can seriously affect our moods, thought patterns, and physical wellbeing.

1. **Check any of the following signs of depression that apply to you:**
    - **Persistent negative thoughts**
    - **A sense of helplessness**
    - **A sense of hopelessness**
    - **Lack of motivation**
    - **Trouble concentrating or paying attention**
    - **Persistent guilt**
    - **Persistent sadness or crying**
    - **Irritation at small things**
    - **A decrease in pleasure in the things you once enjoyed**
    - **Increase or decrease in appetite and weight**
    - **Trouble sleeping or waking up**
    - **Low energy levels**
    - **Feelings of heaviness in your arms and legs**
    - **Headaches**
    - **Constipation**
    - **General aches and pains**

2. **Considering your response to the above list of symptoms, how would you rate yourself in terms of depression?**
    - **I am not at all depressed**
    - **I may be experiencing some depression**

- I am depressed a lot of the time
- I am very depressed
- I am so depressed that life seems completely hopeless

3. Have you experienced depression before, or is this the first time? Do you suspect that your abortion might have contributed to your depression?

As with fear and anxiety, just knowing that you are working on the underlying causes of emotional distress can be helpful and motivate you to carry on. However, if your depression has become debilitating, it may be necessary to consult your medical doctor for help.

4. Select responses from this passage to counteract the following thoughts of a depressed person, as in the example given.

I have called you back from the ends of the earth so you can serve me, for I have chosen you and will not throw you away. Don't be afraid, for I am with you. Don't be dismayed, for I am your God. I will strengthen you. I will help you. I will uphold you with my victorious right hand.

Isaiah 41:9-10

FEAR	PROMISE
• I am too far gone	*I have called you back from the ends of the earth*
• I am bewildered	
• I have no resources	
• I am scared	
• I am useless	
• I have no stamina	
• I am lonely	
• I am worthless	
• I deserve to go to hell	
• I feel powerless	

5. **Consult the ideas below if you need help counteracting depression:**

    - Eat three healthy meals a day and three healthy snacks.

    - Drink 8 glasses of water.

    - Avoid caffeine, sugar, junk food, and alcohol.

    - Make an appointment to see your doctor if necessary.

    - Take prescribed medications.

    - Exercise at least 30 minutes, preferably in fresh air and daylight.

    - Take a shower, do your hair, put on some lipstick, and wear an attractive outfit.

    - Spend 20 minutes praying, meditating, or journaling.

    - Do something fun or creative: plan activities that you will anticipate enjoying.

    - Keep in touch with family and friends.

    - Try to go to work.

    - Make a To Do List including tasks such as shopping for groceries, housework, watering plants, and walking the dog. Check items off as you do them to give yourself a sense of accomplishment.

6. **Write a short reflection on how depression may be clouding your life.   Finish with an action plan.**

COPING STRATEGIES

In the past you may have tried all sorts of ways of handling the pain and stress that followed your abortion. It is common, when pain or stress build to a certain level, to seek relief in whatever form it may come. However, the use of coping strategies eventually leads to a deep restlessness and a sense that your life is out of control. Ignoring these warning signals results in denial; denial creates more stress; the stress then drives you back to the coping behavior and a repeat of the cycle.

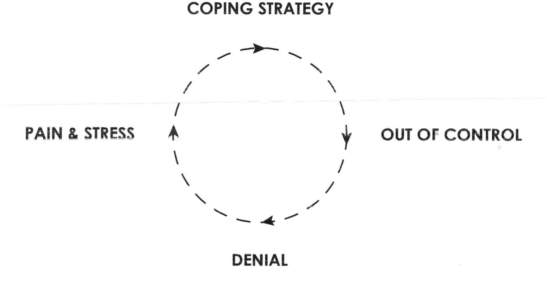

COPING STRATEGY

PAIN & STRESS   **OUT OF CONTROL**

DENIAL

1. **Highlight any of the following coping strategies that apply to you:**

    Pain numbing through
    *   abuse of alcohol
    *   abuse of drugs
    *   abuse of food (eating disorders)
    *   dressing/grooming perfectly
    *   being a perfect Christian
    *   have a replacement baby

    Self-punishment by
    *   cutting
    *   self-sabotaging behaviors
    *   denial of enjoyable experiences
    *   being in abusive relationships
    *   neglect of personal health
    *   neglect of personal appearance

Compensation by trying to
- be a perfect student
- be a perfect mother/wife
- have a perfect career
- have a perfect home/garden

Distraction of
- workaholism
- gambling
- over-control of people or situations
- shopping
- sex
- passionate pro-life or pro-choice
- involvement

Escape into
- rage
- depression
- suicidal thinking
- technology

Flight from
- mate
- children
- job
- responsibilities
- place

Other?

2.   **Make a note of any of the above examples that come as a surprise to you, whether you have used them yourself or not.**

3. Try to remember whether you have experienced the cycle shown in the preceding diagram. Describe what happened when you used one of your coping strategies to try to relieve your stress and pain.

4. Read how Andrea's coping strategy, following her abortion, impacted her life.

Andrea was an intelligent woman who believed passionately in justice. In fact, she became a lawyer so that she could make things as fair as possible for as many people as possible. Then Andrea had an abortion.

She knew that what she had done was wrong and felt that she deserved a life sentence. However, she was free in the eyes of the justice system. So Andrea tried to make things as fair as she could by remaining in an abusive relationship for ten years. She felt that was appropriate punishment for her actions.

Although everyone kept telling her that she deserved a healthier relationship, she felt that she knew better; she was getting exactly what she deserved.

5. Andrea's coping strategy was self-punishment. What have you learned about how your own coping strategies have impacted your life?

6. You are now working to heal your pain and relieve your stress. How do you think this focus and effort will affect your own use of coping strategies?

WHO AM I NOW?

Compare the kind of person you are now with who you were before your abortion experience. As you assess how your abortion has affected you, make it your goal to heal in such a way that you have all the potential of that "before" person, combined with the courage and insight that your recovery can inspire.

1.   **What is my home life like now? Has it changed since the abortion?**

2.   **How am I relating to my parents, brothers, and sisters? Are we as close as we once were?**

3.   **What kind of student or employee am I? Could I be doing better?**

4.   **How are my friendships? Am I spending time with friends who bring out the best in me?**

5.   **Am I still passionate about the sports or hobbies that I was involved in before?**

6.   **Refer back to chapter two and the exercise WHO WAS I? Look at the words you used to describe yourself then and record whether they are different now.**

7.   Have my greatest strengths and weaknesses changed at all?

8.   What role is God/faith playing in my life today?

9.   How healthy is my dating or marriage relationship? Or am I fulfilled as a single?

10. Would someone who knew me well before the abortion now change their former description of me?

TAKE CARE OF YOURSELF

Grieving requires a vast amount of energy. Many women mistakenly think that grieving entails sackcloth and ashes, fasting, and sleepless nights. This is a foolish and unsuccessful way to proceed.

Grieving is not an exercise in masochism. Don't expect to be able to tolerate your grief if you don't eat or sleep. Don't attempt to confront your grief if you are not taking optimal care of your health. Part of your commitment to recovery involves a commitment to your own health.

In the past, you may have neglected your own personal needs because you felt you deserved to suffer. Now you must get plenty of rest. Embrace a healthy, nutritious diet, and exercise. Physical activity will decrease depression, help you sleep, and release endorphins that will enable you to relax.

Allow your journey towards healing to be a time of inner transformation. It is a time to be good to yourself and treat yourself with gentleness.

No matter what has happened in your life, you are created in the image and likeness of God. He created you for a great good, and He will help to restore you when you feel broken and worn down.

You can use your gifts, talents, and experiences ~ including even your most painful experiences ~ for the good of yourself and others. When you have finished all your grief work, you will have a depth of understanding and compassion that will make you more effective in helping others.

It is true that much good can come out of a bad experience. It is your job now to take care of yourself so that you can find that goodness and begin sharing it with those you love.[4]

Theresa Burke

Think about how well you are taking care of yourself these days. Note at least three reasons why you are worth taking care of:

---

4   Theresa Burke with David C. Reardon *Forbidden Grief: The Unspoken Pain of Abortion* (Springfield, IL: Acorn Books 2002) pgs 254-255. Reprinted and used by permission.

CUTTING & STICKING

Pictures can help us process our emotions. Still, what may seem instinctive to some can feel awkward to others. If you are reluctant to do this exercise, give it a try nonetheless: you may be surprised by how well it works!

Using the space below, or a larger piece of scrapbook paper, create a collage of pictures (and words, if you like) that illustrates a topic from this chapter.

CHAPTER FOUR

VOLCANIC ACTIVITY

VOLCANIC ACTIVITY

Volcanic activity is a response to the build-up of pressure below the surface. We are most familiar with images of a violent eruption of fiery lava and clouds of ash that block out the sun. However, there are other means of release: a steady escape of scalding steam, or the intermittent seepage of lava from the side of the volcano.

Anger is much the same. Although angry people often do erupt physically or verbally, there are also those who steam beneath the surface or vent in less obvious ways. Perhaps they are uncomfortable with open displays of emotion; maybe they were raised to believe that the expression of anger is inappropriate. This doesn't mean that they are not angry—they have just found other ways of releasing it!

This chapter deals with the anger, triggers, and anniversary reactions that are all connected to our pain and stress. You will learn to recognize and understand anger in general, and to identify your personal anger patterns and outcomes. Most importantly, you will assemble tools that will be useful for a lifetime.

Suppressed anger brewed beneath the surface of my emotions, causing
the roots of bitterness to grow deep in my heart. Unfortunately, it was those closest to me
who suffered from the outbursts, depression, and drug abuse.

Joan Phillips

ANGER EXPLAINED

Anger is a complex and poorly understood emotion that can play havoc with our lives. Author and pastoral care counselor David Augsburger cautions us to treat it with respect:

> *With such a spread from the frigidity of hate to the fever of rage, the emotion of anger should be one of our best understood, most carefully managed, and most effectively channeled emotions. It is much too powerful to be overlooked, much too dangerous to be ignored.* [5]

Anger can manifest in many ways, and in varying degrees. At one end of the spectrum is righteous anger, a natural response to injustice or wrongdoing. At the other end is the toxic anger that frequently arises due to unresolved pain or frustration. This kind of anger, if left unattended, can lead to lasting harm to us and to others.

Abortion and the circumstances surrounding it create a fertile breeding ground for anger. We may be angry at God, ourselves, our partners, family, friends, the law, medical personnel, contraception that failed, and so on.

In order to heal, we must come to terms with our anger and gain skills that will allow us to deal with it in life-giving ways. One of the first steps involves identifying how we typically deal with our anger. Here are three possibilities:

SUPPRESSION involves avoiding any expression of our anger. Although this tactic may seem noble, prolonged suppression can be dangerous both emotionally and physically.

REPRESSION occurs when people ignore and deny their anger to such a degree that they are unable to express it, or even acknowledge it to themselves. To block and deny what you are experiencing is to live a lie. For example, while I may truly believe that I am not angry, the fact that I constantly grind my teeth while sleeping suggests otherwise.

EXPRESSION

> *Explosion* is the most familiar hallmark of anger. It is the outward eruption of anger towards others, God, institutions, or inanimate objects. This form of anger is evident in
> - bullying
> - venting
> - shouting, screaming, and cursing
> - aggression

5   David Augsburger *The Freedom of Forgiveness* (Chicago: The Moody Bible Institute 1970, 1988)

- assault
- abuse
- violence
- destruction

Implosion is anger expressed inwardly, towards the self. It can surface as

- self-loathing
- self-sabotage
- a sense of unworthiness
- a tendency to put oneself down
- isolation from others or an attempt to keep emotional distance
- a tendency to become a doormat
- a tendency to sabotage relationships
- rebellion
- dangerous sexual activity
- digestive issues such as ulcers, colitis, and stomach problems
- heart problems, high blood pressure
- headaches
- chronic exhaustion
- depression
- weakening of the immune system

Other ways anger can be expressed include

- irritability
- impatience
- snappishness
- touchiness or sensitivity
- bad temper
- sarcasm
- habitual lateness
- bitterness
- hatred
- hostility

1. Highlight any of the anger responses that apply to you. Then plot where you believe your anger ranks on the line below.

    Not angry   Extremely angry

2. Now consider anger in terms of color.

Red:	The quick flash of scalding anger
Purple:	Congested, inhibited, internalized anger
Blue:	Depressed and despairing anger
Black:	Destructive wrath
White:	A cold, calculating desire for annihilation

    As you review these descriptions and your responses above, what color would you most associate with your anger?

3. Did you inherit or learn your anger style from anyone in particular as you were growing up? Who was it? How did this person's anger affect you?

4. How would someone who knows you well describe you when you are angry?

5. How do others react when you are angry?

6.   **How has your anger affected your relationships?**

- **at home**

- **socially**

- **at school/work**

7.   **Has your abortion experience changed your anger style from what it was before?**

At the core of all anger is a need that is not being fulfilled.
Marshall B. Rosenberg

ANGER IN ACTION

Anger is a fascinating emotion: although it has enabled humans to survive in life-threatening circumstances, it can also erupt over something as trivial as a missing set of keys or a long wait in a traffic jam. Although we express anger in different ways, each of us tends to follow a predictable four-stage process.

A TRIGGER IS ACTIVATED:	Words, an experience, a memory, a person, a situation, or a place can cause a spark, commonly called a "trigger."
EMOTIONS ARE AROUSED:	Feelings such as frustration, fear, embarrassment, loss of control, hurt, shame or abandonment flood the heart and mind.
ENERGY SURGES:	The nervous system tells the body to prepare for "fight or flight." Many dramatic physiological responses take place almost instantaneously: levels of adrenaline rise, the heart rate increases, blood vessels constrict, and the resulting rush of blood to the muscles prepares them for action.
REACTION OCCURS:	The natural response to this emotional and physical arousal is to use our programmed behaviors, such as shouting, cursing, striking, or slamming doors, to act out our anger.

Unfortunately, this progression can be as quick as a flash, and we often fail to realize that our feelings and physical responses have even been involved. It seems that as soon as our fuse is lit, we launch into reaction. Understanding the whole process—that anger is more than a knee-jerk response—is the beginning of controlling it.

1. **Refer back to ANGER EXPLAINED and try to identify your anger style. Are you a represser, suppresser, exploder, imploder, or other?**

2. **Think of a time in the past couple of weeks when you became angry. What set you off? How did you react?**

TAMING ANGER

To gain control over our anger, we essentially need to work backwards through the stages of its development. Anger is a *secondary* emotion; it does not appear out of nowhere, but rather is a reaction to the triggering of emotional pain.

STOP THE REACTION:	Pause before anger carries you away into behavior you may regret.
REDIRECT YOUR ENERGY:	Choose a non-destructive method to use up the surge of energy.
EXAMINE YOUR HEART:	Look for the underlying feelings that led to this powerful physiological response.
IDENTIFY THE TRIGGER:	Understand what set the whole anger response into motion and respond, this time, with controlled and appropriate action.

A significant part of keeping anger in check involves separating our physical arousal from our emotional arousal. Feelings always underlie anger, but before we can calm down enough to examine our hearts, we must find ways to use up the surge of energy.

Healthy options may include physical activities such as running or taking part in an acceptably aggressive sport such squash or an hour at the golf driving range. Using a punching bag or pillow, playing a musical instrument loudly, breathing deeply, or even finding a secluded place to shout or scream can also release energy.

Then, having siphoned off that toxic energy, we can attend to our feelings by thinking, praying, talking, writing, creating a collage, drawing, painting, or listening to music that gives expression to our pain. This contemplation must be done thoroughly and well because only then will we be free to move past our anger to its healing conclusion—forgiveness.

1. **Highlight the anger guidelines contained in these verses.**

   Psalm 4:4 ~ Don't sin by letting anger gain control over you. Think about it overnight and remain silent.

   Proverbs 29:11 ~ A fool gives full vent to anger, but a wise person quietly holds it back.

Proverbs 14:17a ~ Those who are short-tempered do foolish things.

Romans 12:19 ~ Dear friends, never avenge yourselves. Leave that to God. For it is written, I will take vengeance; I will repay those who deserve it, says the Lord.

2. **Note activities you might choose to use up the *surge of energy* that accompanies your anger:**

3. **Which of the suggestions mentioned would feel most natural as you process the *feelings* that lie beneath your anger? Have you used any of these methods before? Can you give an example?**

4. **On extra paper, draw or use images from magazines to remind yourself of ways to use up a surge of unwanted energy. On another page, do the same to show how you could process your wounded emotions.**

ANGER CASE STUDY

Last night Megan allowed her teenage son, Jake, to use her car. Everyone in the family has left for the day and Megan is ready to run out the door, with no time to spare, for an important meeting. She goes to grab her car keys only to discover that they're not on the hook by the door.

Megan mutters a few choice obscenities, and then remembers how Jake had flopped his gangly, oversized body onto the couch after he came home. Careening into the family room, she flings cushions, magazines, and TV controllers around as she frantically searches for her keys.

She then tears upstairs and strides into his bedroom to search his desk and bedside tables. She digs fruitlessly through the pockets of his jeans, shirt, and hoodie. The chewing tobacco and condom she finds in his pockets inflame her further and she takes grim pleasure in throwing his clothes around the room. Megan is so worked up that she finds herself wishing that there was something—preferably large and weighty—to throw that would make a really satisfying crash.

Infuriated by the knowledge that she will now be late for her meeting and may lose her job (and her career along with it), Megan is ready to gag on her frustration. Her carefully put together outfit, hair, and make-up are showing the effects of her frenzy.

Not knowing where to look next or what to do, she stands in the centre of Jake's room, breathing heavily. Skinning her son alive comes to mind: she pauses to relish the thought.

As she does, she thinks back to last night and the playful way he called out his thanks for the use of her car as he lobbed her keys across the kitchen to her. With a groan, Megan remembers telling herself to hang them back on the key hook as she laid them down beside the kitchen sink.

1.   **What lit Megan's fuse?**

2.   **What feelings do you think the missing keys aroused in her?**

3.   **What reactions did the surge of energy set off?**

4. What exactly happened that allowed Megan the clarity to remember where her keys were?

5. How could Megan have cut short her progression of anger immediately after discovering that her keys were missing?

6. How do you think she felt after this event?

7. What can Megan do to prevent a repeat of this experience?

8. Have you had a similar kind of experience?

9. Can you recognize the "fuse-feelings-energy-action" progression?

10. In the future, do you think you will be able to defuse a situation before it develops? How will you remember what you have learned?

Anger is something we feel. It exists for a reason and always deserves our respect and attention.
Harriet Goldhor Lerner

ANGER EXCERPTS

Joanna knew about anger. She had been jailed for 5 years as a result of taking a loaded shotgun and threatening to kill the people she was most angry at, and then herself. She believed that being angry made her strong. It had the added bonus of distracting her from thinking about all the losses in her tragic life. Joanna believed that crying or grieving made you weak, so she made sure to avoid that by staying as angry as possible.
~ Anon

Hate is as all-absorbing as love, as irrational, and in its own way as satisfying...
The major difference between hating and loving is perhaps that whereas to love somebody is to be fulfilled and enriched by the experience, to hate somebody is to be diminished and drained by it. Lovers, by losing themselves in their loving, find themselves, become themselves. Haters simply lose themselves. Theirs is the ultimate consuming passion.[6]
~ Frederick Buechner

I had killed three babies: once I acknowledged that fact, my anger toward those involved in my abortions was intense. I thought of Bob and Chuck and my anger burned. How could they have put me in that position? I thought of those professionals who performed the abortions and I fumed. How could they have lied to me? Why didn't they tell me the truth about fetal development? I began with the doctor, pouring out my rage on paper, detailing every point of my fury, addressing him by name. Then I wrote to Bob and then Chuck. Letter after letter I wrote, until I had exhausted every person and every reason for anger my heart could dredge up. It took time and energy to uncover the depth of emotion I had toward so many people. But letter by letter, person by person, the anger seemed to subside. Though never mailed, the result of the letters was a heavy burden released and, finally, peace.[7]
~ Joan Phillips

Read these excerpts several times. Then write a reflection on the cost of rage, fury, and hatred, and the benefits of confronting these toxic feelings. Use extra paper if necessary.

6   Frederick Buechner *Whistling In The Dark: An ABC Theologized* (San Francisco: Harper & Row, 1988)
7   Copyright 1998 Cook Communications Ministries. <u>Her Choice to Heal</u> by Sydna Masse and Joan Phillips. Used by permission. May not be further reproduced. All rights reserved.

ANGER PIE

1. Think about your anger that is connected to your abortion experience. You may be angry with people, institutions, medical personnel, God, etc. Make a list of the targets of your anger:

2. Now divide the pie into slices representing the proportion of anger you feel towards each target.

ANGER PIE

WHAT NEXT?

Go back a couple of pages and read Joan's passage from ANGER EXCERPTS again, slowly and carefully. Put yourself in her shoes: feel her fury, followed by the surge of energy that drove her to write all her letters. Then try to imagine the relief and peace she experienced after her letter writing had moved her anger out of her heart and onto the page.

Now it's your turn. Remember the suggestions mentioned in the past few pages: stop before you do something you may regret, siphon off the energy, identify the hurts, and process the feelings.

1. **If you need to do some siphoning of energy before or during this exercise, jog on the spot, windmill your arms, or do some solitary shouting.**

2. **Take each segment of your Anger Pie and identify, one by one, how your anger targets have hurt you emotionally and physically, or in another way.**

3. **Don't hesitate to keep an entire stack of paper at hand for this exercise—you will need plenty of room to vent. Write a letter to each target using the format below. Repeat this process until you have covered all of your anger targets. Do not hold back: anger is poisoning you, and this is a way of getting it out of your life. Use this opportunity to really "let 'er rip"!**

    PLEASE NOTE: YOU WILL NOT BE SENDING THESE LETTERS

    To _____ ,
        I am angry with you because...

4. **Writing anger letters is exhausting. Once you have finished, you might enjoy a long, peaceful soak in the bathtub with candles and soothing music. Relax and connect with how you feel now that those toxic feelings have moved out of your heart, down your arm, and onto the paper. Go to bed with your journal and pen on the bedside table. When you wake up, record how you are feeling.**

5. **After writing all of your anger letters, read them aloud, preferably to a trusted person. If such a person is not available, even reading aloud to the wall is beneficial. There is something powerful about the process of writing and reading aloud: some would even describe it as a supernatural remedy for a damaged soul.**

6.   Only after this is done will you decide what to do with the letters. You may need to keep them for a while and re-read them from time to time, or you may shred, burn, bury, or throw them into the ocean.

Write a short prayer or ceremonial words that you might use as you dispose of your anger letters.

TRIGGERS

A trigger is a reminder of some past event that intrudes on the present and arouses various physical, mental, and emotional responses. Triggers may be pleasant, such as the aroma of cookies baking that reminds us of a visit to grandma's house. They may also be extremely distressing, such as the wet sucking sound at the bottom of a slurpee cup that brings abortion-related sounds back to vivid life.

Triggers may be seen, heard, smelled, felt, or tasted. They may be a place, person, occasion, weather, piece of clothing, or something you read. The unpleasant or frightening responses to triggers include:

- flashbacks
- spacing out
- anxiety
- hyper-ventilation
- fear
- anger or rage
- dizziness
- confusion
- numbness
- nausea
- shakiness
- full-blown panic attacks

Triggers are uniquely personal and have the power to create havoc. When a trigger related to a traumatic event is experienced, our adrenal glands are stimulated. The stress hormones adrenaline and cortisol enter the bloodstream, activating emotional and physical responses that may include memories.

When a memory is activated, we may experience a flashback that takes us back to the traumatic event. Sometimes, however, seemingly random physical and emotional responses appear to come out of nowhere and possess a life of their own, resulting in a particularly terrifying experience.

Fortunately, triggers can be defused and responses brought under control. The following strategies may prove effective:

1. Keep a list of each trigger and note in your journal what you can recall about the experience. Ask yourself when, where, who, why, and how questions, and record as much detail as possible, including time, weather, sounds, smells, atmosphere, your level of stress, etc.

Record how you respond to each one. Then choose coping strategies: your newfound awareness and preparation will enable you to manage future triggers and responses more effectively.

2. Plan your strategies and choose to

- Ignore the trigger by refusing to grant it any power over you
- Confront the trigger by looking it in the eye and telling it where to go!
- Distract yourself by whistling, turning up the music, or moving briskly
- Redirect your thoughts by focusing intently on something else, or by engaging in a healthy hobby or physical activity
- Calm yourself by using deep breathing, prayer, relaxation exercises, or visualization of MY SAFE PLACE described in the second chapter
- Place yourself firmly back in the present
- Record your trigger, responses, and coping methods in your journal

CONFRONTING YOUR TRIGGERS

1. Just for some light relief, choose a trigger that brings back pleasant memories. Briefly describe it and the feelings it recalls. The fresh scent of pine trees may bring to mind an energizing mountain hike, for example, and the pleasure of a day spent in the company of close friends.

2. Some of the triggers that are common after abortion are listed below. Highlight those that have caused you distress. Add any others that you have also experienced.

    *   Self-centered men
    *   Men in general
    *   Being pressured while feeling confused
    *   Not being heard
    *   Feeling powerless
    *   Waiting rooms
    *   Disinfectant/antiseptic odors
    *   Medical personnel
    *   Gynecological examinations
    *   Sounds of vacuum cleaners
    *   Wet, slurping sounds
    *   Sexual intimacy
    *   Menstrual cramps
    *   Pregnant women
    *   Fetal development pictures
    *   Movies about childbirth
    *   Babies and/or baby items
    *   Pro-life or pro-choice propaganda
    *   Fear of others finding out
    *   Anniversary dates
    *   Other?
    *   Other?

3.   Place an "A" beside triggers you already knew were connected to your abortion experience. Place an "N" beside triggers you now know are connected to your abortion experience.

4.   Choose one of your most troublesome triggers. Describe in detail the mental, physical, and/or emotional responses it has caused. Ask yourself   when, where, why, who, and how, as well as providing details, such as the weather, your level of stress, sounds, smells, etc.

5.   The previous notes on triggers suggest strategies for defusing a trigger reaction: ignore, confront, distract, redirect, calm, place, and record.

   •   Write a script of a few sentences that you would use to confront and reject a trigger you have experienced.

   •   Choose a tune to whistle, hum, or sing that gives you a feeling of confidence and strength.

   •   Consider what activity involves your complete attention and effort and could be used to distract you from a troublesome trigger. Note it here.

   •   Practice deep breathing. Describe another technique for relaxation, if you have one.

- Bring to mind the safe place that you described in chapter two, and visualize it when distressed by a trigger. Record the name of your safe place here.

- Write a script that you can use to place yourself in the here and now.

6. Create a list of triggers, including those you identified in chapter one, in your journal. Describe your reactions and your strategies for coping. Add more triggers as you identify them, knowing that "naming them is more than halfway to taming them"!

KNOWING WHAT I KNOW NOW

When you go back and actively remember your abortion experience, you will often wish that you had done things differently. Here is your opportunity. Choose the situations below that apply to you, altering them or adding to them when necessary. Record your responses... knowing what you know now.

1. When the father of the baby said, "If you want to keep that kid, I'm out of here!" or words to that effect, what do you wish you had said to him?

2. When the father of the baby said, "It's going to ruin my (or your) life/schooling/career/reputation/future if you have that baby!", how would you respond now?

3. When you refused to acknowledge that what you were carrying was actually a child, what do you wish you had done instead?

4. When you, or someone trying to assure you, said, "It's just a clump of cells," what information would you rely on now?

5. When your parents or friends said, "What will people think? There's no other way—you've got to have an abortion!", how could you have responded?

6. When your girlfriend said, "Oh, I've had an abortion—it's no big deal," what could you tell her now?

7. When the clinic personnel told you that you might be sad for a couple of weeks, but then you'd get over it, what truth do you wish they had shared?

8. Add your own situations and responses as needed.

ANNIVERSARY REACTIONS

Anniversary reactions are responses to a date connected to an abortion experience. Typically emotional, but sometimes physical, these responses are a classic example of a post-abortion trigger. The anniversary isn't necessarily a specific day: it could be a period of time such as early September or spring, and it may generate reactions such as those listed in number three below.

1.   **Do you remember the date of your abortion? Record your best recollection here.**

2.   **Have you had emotional reactions around any of the following times? Highlight any that apply.**

     •   **Anniversary of date of abortion**

     •   **Anniversary of abandonment by partner, or other loss related to abortion**

     •   **Anniversary of expected date of delivery**

     •   **Mother's Day (a day that can also trigger an anniversary reaction)**

3.   **Highlight any of the following you may have noticed around the time of an abortion-related anniversary.**

     •   **Preoccupation with thoughts of the abortion**

     •   **Agitation or anxiety**

     •   **Hopelessness or powerlessness**

     •   **Sadness**

     •   **Depression**

     •   **Anger**

     •   **Nightmares**

     •   **Inability to concentrate**

     •   **Relationship conflicts**

     •   **Thoughts of harming oneself**

     •   **Becoming accident prone**

     •   **Abdominal cramping**

     •   **General sense of feeling unwell**

     •   **Other?**

4.   **Can you describe in detail an anniversary reaction you have had, now that you know what it was?**

5.   **Have you been afraid of an anniversary date related to your abortion in the past—afraid, in particular, of what it might unleash? Are you anxious about future anniversary dates?**

6.   **Have you felt powerless in the face of that fear? Explain.**

Half of the challenge of managing your anniversary reactions is identifying what is going on. The rest of the process involves creating a plan to counteract any emotional upheavals. By doing so you are choosing to be pro-active rather than reactive. Once you are armed for the confrontation, reactions typically lessen over time.

ANNIVERSARY ACTION PLAN

Divide the day in half. Use the morning to *honor your child* and the afternoon to *honor yourself*. Plan to include God in your day by inviting his comfort, strength, and healing power into each activity.

MORNING: Focus on your child. Pray as you invite your child into your consciousness. Allow yourself to imagine your child as he or she might have looked. If you have a name for your child, use it as you visualize. Cry if you need to, journal your thoughts and feelings, write a letter to your child, make a collage about your child at the age he or she would be now, visit a meaningful place, make a donation to an organization that honors children, play music that speaks to your heart, etc.

AFTERNOON: Commit to living the life that your child would want for you. Buy yourself flowers, journal, pray, write a letter to yourself, feel loved and worthy. Examine your healing: is there any further work that needs doing? Exercise, go out and have fun, get together with a friend, watch a funny movie, take a long soak in the tub with candles and soothing music, journal some more, and then crawl into bed having conquered the dragon!

---

7. How do you feel now that you know what an anniversary reaction is and what you can do about it? Does this knowledge lessen your fear of facing dates that might trigger a reaction?

8. In preparation for a troublesome anniversary, imagine how you would spend your day. Take a separate sheet of paper and use pictures or words to describe how you would honor your child, and how you would honor yourself.

When we grieve our losses to completion, we grow.

Charles L. Whitfield

ANNIVERSARY CASE STUDY

Carly completed her post-abortion healing program six months before the anniversary of her abortion. A few weeks before the anniversary date, she went to see her counselor, as she was feeling flat and hopeless. She remembered learning about triggers and wondered whether the anniversary was to blame for her depression. Her counselor suggested using the Anniversary Action Plan to handle the day. Here is her story:

After we last spoke, I did spend a day just as my counselor suggested. I spent the morning writing letters to Ella (my child) and to those I am ready to forgive. In the afternoon, I went out and got my hair done (something for me) and spent some time talking on the phone with my fiancé, Ryan, about my letters. In the evening, I went to a girlfriend's house to watch a movie and relax. It was a very nice day.

On the actual anniversary date, I had flown to visit Ryan. He promised to spend the day with me since it had fallen on a Saturday. Unfortunately, he got called in for work and was only able to spend the later afternoon with me. It turned out to be good, though, because I got to spend the morning writing, and reflecting, a bit more than I had the first time.

I had a difficult time writing and was pretty upset, but I wrote about the events that occurred the day of the abortion. It was the first time I had done that since the post-abortion healing program. When Ryan finished work, he took me to the beach.

The sun had just gone down when we got there and the waves were crashing like crazy. We were on a beach near a naval base and there was some heavy artillery being shot off in the distance. . .it was quite dramatic. Ryan and I sat huddled on the beach to keep warm and I read my letters to him. We said a prayer. Then we tied the letters to a big rock, and Ryan threw them into the crashing waves. As I watched the rock hit the waves, I felt relief and happiness in so many ways.

Afterwards, Ryan and I got take-out and watched a movie together. It was a really special day, and I finally felt some closure. Thank you so much for your suggestion to celebrate that day in such a way. Even though it was hard and upsetting, it certainly was worth it, and when I think about it, I think of it as a good day.

PLEASE NOTE: Your actual anniversary date may fall on a day that you are working or occupied and unable to carry out the Anniversary Action Plan. Just do as Carly did and dedicate a different day to deal with your anniversary reactions. When the actual anniversary day arrives, do something to put your stamp of healing on that date, as she did, so that a day of conflict becomes a day of closure instead. Used by permission.

WHY DIDN'T GOD STOP ME?

Sometimes we wonder why God allowed us to take the path that led to our abortion and its agonizing aftermath. Perhaps, at such a time, it would be helpful to stand back and look at our lives from his perspective.

H.H. Farmer once said: *If you go against the grain of the universe, you are going to get splinters.* Try to keep his wisdom in mind as you continue to read this passage.

A new appliance always comes with a "Use and Care Manual," and we have a choice to read it and follow its advice. If we follow the guidelines, we can be reasonably assured that the appliance will perform well and last a long time.

Likewise, God, who created us, provided us with a detailed "Use and Care Manual" to follow for our safety, health, and happiness. This manual, otherwise known as the Bible, clearly states that sex outside of marriage is forbidden. The same holds true for the shedding of innocent blood.

We have each done at least one of these things. Obviously the one who clearly forbids something is not at the same time going to tempt us to do it. That is our own doing. As James 1:13-14 states,

> No one who wants to do wrong should ever say, "God is tempting me." God is never tempted to do wrong, and he never tempts anyone else either. Temptation comes from the lure of our own evil desires. These evil desires lead to evil actions, and evil actions lead to death.

Along with the Bible's clear guidelines, we have also been given the power to make choices. Unfortunately, it is a fact of life that one unhealthy choice can set us on a slippery slope, leaving us vulnerable to slipping further and further into darkness.

The vast majority of today's media messages promote the idea that we can engage in sex without consequences. But we have learned from bitter experience that this is not true. Each of us has faced a pregnancy that has placed us in a precarious situation. When we chose abortion, we slid further down the slippery slope.

But all is not lost. Although God certainly cannot be blamed for getting us there, he is not going to leave us alone in a crumpled heap. He is waiting to rescue us from the chaos of our own poor choices. He aches to hear us cry out to him for forgiveness. And he longs to give us the healing, peace, and restoration that accompany it.

As long as we are alive, we still have a chance to stop, cry out to God, change direction, and start going with the grain of the universe. And we can confidently trust God to take care of the splinters!

Have you wondered why God didn't stop you? Reflect on this passage, and record what you have learned. Write a one-sentence statement that summarizes what you now know.

CHOICES

Life involves a series of choices, and all of our choices—whether momentous or insignificant, measured or careless—play a role in forming us as people. We become who we are in increments, each choice molding us into a person of finer or lesser character.

In his timeless classic *Mere Christianity*, C.S. Lewis notes that our decisions are slowly transforming us

> into a heavenly creature or into a hellish creature: either into a creature that is in harmony with God, and with other creatures, and with itself, or else into one that is in a state of war and hatred with God, and with its fellow creatures, and with itself.

Some choices—such as the decision to abort—have the power to change us into beings of rage, powerlessness, self-loathing, and despair. And yet subsequent choices have the power to do quite the opposite. Every choice that turns us into a more "heavenly creature" also moves us towards a life of wholeness, hope, power, and peace[8]

Read this excerpt several times, highlighting the parts that capture your attention. Think about the choices you have when dealing with your anger. What decisions can you make that will enable you to embrace "joy, and peace, and knowledge, and power"?

8   C.S. Lewis *Mere Christianity* (New York: Macmillan Publishing Co., Inc. 1943) p86.

ANGER SUMMARY

1. **What have I learned about anger?**

2. **What are my tools for dealing with anger?**

3. **How can I remember what I have learned about anger?**

4. **Create a collage, here or on a separate sheet, that illustrates any aspect of what you have learned about your anger.**

Anger is our friend. Not a nice friend. Not a gentle friend. But a very, very loyal friend...
It will always tell us that it is time to act in our own best interests.

Julia Cameron

CHAPTER FIVE

FINDING WINGS

FINDING WINGS

So far we have worked painstakingly through the damage caused by our abortion decisions, and we have learned many techniques for dealing with the fallout. But there is one enormous step we can take that has the power to sweep away the wreckage and truly change our lives, and that is forgiveness. With your efforts, this chapter has the potential to be the tipping point in your healing.

Forgiveness was created by God, and it was God who sacrificed his own son, Jesus, to pay the price for our sinfulness. The apostle Paul says in 1 Timothy 1:15b-16,

> *Christ Jesus came into the world to save sinners ~ and I was the worst of them all. But that is why God had mercy on me, so that Christ Jesus could use me as a prime example of his great patience with even the worst sinners. Then others will realize that they, too, can believe in him and receive eternal life.*

Forgiveness doesn't stop with us: it is intended to flow through us and on to those whom we need to forgive. As we receive forgiveness, it is our responsibility to forgive those who have hurt us. This responsibility may offend our sense of justice because we want those who have hurt us to pay—big time! But hanging on to bitterness and refusing to forgive can only make our hearts twisted and ugly. Meanwhile, the one who did the damage—the one who deserves to pay, in our minds—goes merrily on his way.

Accepting forgiveness and extending forgiveness to others is difficult to do. However, our gains will far outweigh our efforts. God speaks of the potential life-changing transformation when he says, in Isaiah 1:18,

> *Come let's talk this over...no matter how deep the stain of your sins, I can remove it. I can make you as clean as freshly fallen snow. Even if you are stained as red as crimson, I can make you as white as wool.*

If you think you can, you can. And if you think you can't, you're right.

Mary Kay Ash

LET'S MAKE A DEAL

In order to make amends for our abortions, it is common to seek comfort by making some kind of bargain. A common, though mistaken, belief is that we can take some action that will compensate for what we have done. There are many variations on this theme, but what all bargains do have in common is a complete inability to free us from regret and remorse. In fact, we often feel worse when keeping our end of the bargain fails to bring the peace and relief we expect.

Read examples of such bargains below, keeping in mind that there may be no conscious understanding of the connection between the bargaining activities and abortion remorse.

- **Cynthia's** deal was to never make the mistake of becoming pregnant again. At first she tried avoiding men, but eventually she met and moved in with Brad. Her abortion had been chosen after the failure of her birth control, so she became extra vigilant. Cynthia grimly monitored her contraception and always used more than one method. She lived in constant fear.

- **Natasha** and her high school boyfriend chose abortion in their teens. They married a few years later and had a daughter. However, Natasha felt so unworthy of her gorgeous baby girl that she insisted on having her tubes tied to make sure that she could not be undeservedly blessed a second time. Her deal at such a young age was a long-term solution to the short-term problem of an unresolved abortion loss.

- **Jessica** married and had a baby several years after her abortion. Her deal was to compensate by being the best mother possible. She breastfed her baby, made her own organic baby food, never let her baby out of her sight, and educated herself tirelessly on the best parenting practices. She believed that her diligent efforts would somehow cancel out the tragedy of her first pregnancy outcome. Unfortunately, her relentless efforts only served to make her strung out, exhausted, and resentful.

- **Francine** took the opposite approach. She believed that God would punish her abortion decision by allowing something terrible to happen to her next baby. So she made a deal with herself to keep as emotionally distant as possible. Francine trusted that when the inevitable tragedy struck, she wouldn't feel so devastated. Instead, she lived with a constant sense of estrangement from her little boy.

- **Beth's** deal was to take all of her remorse and regret and use it to fuel her support of the pro-life cause. She promised herself that if she marched, waved placards, and made impassioned speeches, it would all make up for her own devastating choice. Beth became a fierce and vocal advocate, quite unlike the gentle woman she was by nature.

- **Lydia** was determined not to give in to her sense of brokenness after her abortion. Her deal was to become a strident pro-choice promoter in order to validate her own decision. She even encouraged a couple of girlfriends to have abortions. Her lack of peace in the face of these actions simply drove her to greater efforts.

- **Sandra** chose abortion because she felt that an unplanned pregnancy would negatively affect her climb up the corporate ladder. After making such a huge sacrifice, her deal was to make absolutely sure to set herself apart from her colleagues in her commitment and outcomes. However, working day and night for her mega-salary never touched the aching void in her soul.

- **Jane** tried to make a deal with God by becoming pregnant again to prove to him that she could do the right thing next time. But nothing about her circumstances had changed, and the same pressures drove her to abort a second time.

1. **Do any of these case studies seem familiar to you? Why?**

2. **Describe the deals that you have made with yourself, God, or others.**

3. **Have any of your deals brought relief or healing in any way?**

4. **What does it feel like to be powerless over your abortion remorse?**

5. Can you identify what the women in the case studies all need to release them from their deal-making?

6. Have you ever tried to involve God in dealing with your remorse and regret?

7. What can God offer that none of our deal-making can provide?

LOOKING FOR GOD?

So long as we imagine that it is we who have to look for God, then we must often lose heart. But it is the other way about: he is looking for us.

And so, we can afford to recognize that very often we are not looking for God; far from it, we are in full flight from him. And he knows that and has taken it into account.

He has followed us into our own darkness; there where we thought finally to escape him, we run straight into his arms.

God's providence means that wherever we have got to, whatever we have done, that is precisely where the road to heaven begins.

However many cues we have missed, however many wrong turns we have taken, however unnecessarily we may have complicated our journey, the road still beckons, and the Lord still waits to be gracious to us.[9]

Simon Tugwell

1. **How does thinking about God make you feel?**

2. **Have your feelings about God been formed by the influence of someone else, or by your own life experiences? Explain.**

3. **What if God was a critical part of your being forgiven, and being able to forgive others? Are you open to involving God in your forgiveness work?**

4. **After an abortion experience, it is common to feel a profound separation from God, a sense that he has surely written us off. How does it make you feel to know that it is not God who has turned away from you but you who have turned away from him?**

9   Simon Tugwell *Prayer* (Springfield: Templegate Publishers 1975)

5.   It is said that there is no standing still with God. We are always moving *towards* him or away from him. How would you describe what you are doing at this time of your life? Are you comfortable with the direction you have chosen?

6.   Do any phrases in the excerpt speak powerfully to you? Re-write any that have touched your heart, and explain why.

7.   Summarize your feelings about God into one statement and record it here. Repeat your statement aloud several times, trying to sense whether it rings true to you. Is your statement about God likely to help or hinder your recovery?

As surely as I live says the Sovereign Lord, I take no pleasure in the death of wicked people.
I only want them to turn from their wicked ways so they can live. Turn! Turn from your wickedness,
O people of Israel! Why should you die?

Ezekiel 33:11

ANATOMY OF FORGIVENESS

Now that we have examined the fallout from our abortion choices, it is time to confront the most powerful and life changing step of all: forgiveness.

The creation of life is a miraculous and mysterious process by a loving and holy Creator. Those of us who had a relationship with God before our abortions now often turn away from him in shame and anguish. Those of us who have no such relationship simply try to convince ourselves that he doesn't exist and that what he thinks doesn't matter.

Somehow we know, though, the truth that shimmers below the surface of our souls. No matter how much we try to resist the fact, our deepest instincts will eventually bring us to the realization that the only place to turn for forgiveness is to the one who created us and our unborn children.

Refer back to GUILT & SHAME in the third chapter to remind yourself why forgiveness is so important. Here is the process.

CONVICTION:	The unmistakable restlessness and pain of knowing that I have done something wrong.
CONFESSION:	Facing the truth of what I have done and how I feel about it, and then confessing it to God. Needless to say, he already knows all about it but is waiting for me to take ownership and bring my sinfulness before him.
REPENTANCE:	Making a commitment to turning completely away from my sin and refusing to repeat the offence.
ACKNOWLEDGMENT OF AUTHORITY:	Understanding and believing that the death of Jesus paid the price for my sinful deeds, and believing that God has the authority to forgive me and set me free.
REQUEST FOR FORGIVENESS:	Simply asking God to forgive me for my specific sin, once and for all.
FORGIVENESS:	Knowing that I am forgiven completely and utterly, and there is no need to ask again. God has erased my sin.
FORGIVENESS OF OTHERS:	Understanding that forgiveness is a flow-through process and that I am to forgive others as I have been forgiven.

1.   **There are countless verses in the Bible concerning forgiveness. Pick out one or more of the following verses to support each of the forgiveness steps. As you do so, try to allow these truths to settle into your soul. Record the references beside the appropriate headings.**

John 5:24 ~ I tell you the truth, those who listen to my message and believe in God who sent me have eternal life. They will never be condemned for their sins, but they have already passed from death into life.

1 John 1:9 ~ But if we confess our sins to him, he is faithful and just to forgive us and to cleanse us from every wrong.

Psalm 31:9-10 ~ Have mercy on me, Lord, for I am in distress. My sight is blurred because of my tears. My body and soul are withering away. I am dying from grief; my years are shortened by sadness. Misery has drained my strength; I am wasting away from within.

Psalm 6:1-3, 6-7a ~ O Lord, do not rebuke me in your anger or discipline me in your rage. Have compassion on me, Lord, for I am weak. Heal me, Lord, for my body is in agony. I am sick at heart. . . I am worn out from sobbing. Every night tears drench my bed; my pillow is wet from weeping. My vision is blurred with grief.

Proverbs 28:13 ~ People who conceal their sins will not prosper, but if they confess and turn from them, they will receive mercy.

Matthew 6:12 ~ And forgive us our sins just as we have forgiven those who have sinned against us.

Psalm 130:3-4 ~ Lord, if you kept a record of our sins, who, O Lord, could ever survive? But you offer forgiveness, that we might learn to fear (be in awe of) you.

Isaiah 57:15 ~ The high and lofty one who inhabits eternity, the Holy One, says this: "I live in that high and holy place with those whose spirits are contrite and humble. I refresh the humble and give new courage to those with repentant hearts."

Isaiah 44:22 ~ I have swept away your sins like the morning mists. I have scattered your offences like the clouds. Oh, return to me, for I have paid the price to set you free.

Matthew 18:21 ~ Then Peter came to him and asked, "Lord, how often should I forgive someone who sins against me? Seven times?" "No!" Jesus replied, "Seventy times seven!"

Matthew 6: 14-15 ~ If you forgive those who sin against you, your heavenly Father will forgive you. But if you refuse to forgive others, your Father will not forgive your sins.

Psalm 103:12 ~ He has removed our rebellious acts as far as the east is from the west.

Isaiah 43:25 ~ I ~ yes, I alone ~ am the one who blots out your transgressions for my own sake and will remember them no more.

CONVICTION: _____

REPENTANCE: _____

ACKNOWLEDGMENT OF AUTHORITY: _____

REQUEST FOR FORGIVENESS: _____

BEING FORGIVEN: _____

FORGIVENESS OF OTHERS: _____

2. **Which of the above verses is your favorite? Write it out here. Then explain why its truth touches you in a special way.**

3. **Try to memorize your favorite verse, along with its reference. Whenever you are attacked by negative thoughts or feelings, you can conquer them by clearly and firmly repeating the truth to yourself.**

"I have seen what they do, but I will heal them anyway! I will lead them and comfort those who mourn. Then words of praise will be on their lips. May they have peace, both near and far, for I will heal them all," says the Lord.
Isaiah 57:18-19

FORGIVENESS & AUTHORITY

We have a sin problem. We are powerless to help ourselves. Given the right set of circumstances and the wrong state of mind, each of us is capable of just about anything.

I can remember being so devastated over a sin I had allowed to ensnare me that I repeatedly begged God to forgive me. I was repentant the very first time I begged; I confessed my sin with great sorrow and turned radically from it. Still, I continued to plead for forgiveness.

One day God spoke to my heart and said: "Beth, my child, you have an authority problem. You think you can do your part, which is to repent. You just don't think I can do my part, which is to forgive."

I was stunned. I began to realize that my sin of unbelief was as serious as my prior sin of rebellion. I wept and repented for my failure to credit Him with the authority He possessed to forgive my sins. It was eye opening.

My constant re-confessions did not bring me relief. They only made me more miserable and filled me with self-loathing. Relief came when I decided to take God at His Word.

If you have truly repented ~ which means you have experienced godly sorrow and a subsequent detour from the sin ~ bathe yourself in the river of God's forgiveness. Christ has authority to forgive sins right here on earth, you don't have to wait until heaven. You can experience the freedom of complete forgiveness right here, right now. Fall under Christ's authority and accept His grace. You've been paralysed long enough, child of God. Hear Him say to you this day: "Friend, your sins are forgiven...I tell you, get up, take your mat and go home." Luke 5:20, 24 [10]

Beth Moore

Have you also fallen victim to the belief that you need to ask over and over for forgiveness? How does the truth revealed here affect you?

10 Beth Moore *Jesus, the One and Only* (Nashville, Tennessee: Broadman & Holman 2002)

DEAR GOD, IT'S ME...

Many of us will have heard of Judy Blume's book, *Are You There God? It's Me, Margaret*, in which a struggling sixth grader brings up her most pressing issues with God. Although we are no longer young teens struggling with the trials of early adolescence, we are still welcome to bring our intimate questions to God. Here is your opportunity to approach him with your own pressing issues.

1.   **"God-Jesus-Holy Spirit" are all one, so choose which name you feel most comfortable using. How does the thought of talking to God make you feel?**

2.   **Flip back a few pages to the ANATOMY OF FORGIVENESS and use the seven headings as a guide for your own conversation with God. You may like to get started with something along these lines:**

     Dear God,
         I know I haven't spent a lot of time talking to you lately, but I'm starting to think that this anxiety and turmoil over my abortion might have something to do with you trying to get my attention.
         I know what I did was wrong...

3.   **Place two chairs facing each other and sit in one of them. Imagine God sitting opposite. Take your script and read it aloud to him.**

4. **Now, close your eyes and sit quietly as you ask God to speak back to you. Write down what you sense he wants to say to you.**

    My Beloved _____, *(insert your own name)*

5. **Prayer is just this, a conversation between you and God. He is never busy or sleeping, and he longs to hear from you about every detail of your life. Remember to tell him about the good things as well as the sad or difficult, and to trust him with requests for what you need. Always include how thankful you are for what he has done for you. Take a few minutes to write a letter of thanks to God right now.**

    Dear God,
    It is hard to believe that you could love me as much as you do...

He has sent me to tell those who mourn that the time of the Lord's favor has come. . . To all who mourn in Israel, he will give beauty for ashes, joy instead of mourning, praise instead of despair.
Isaiah 61:1a-3a

PRACTICING FORGIVENESS

There is one area of forgiveness that requires no practice at all. This is the asking for, and receiving of, forgiveness from God. Once we have sincerely brought our confession and repentance before God and have asked for forgiveness, it is done. We are forgiven: released from condemnation and punishment and set gloriously free. Not only that, but we have a joyful and abundant future to look forward to—one that will not end with this life.

Since we are only human, God fills our tanks with an unending supply of forgiveness, when we ask. There is a small catch, though: this supply is meant to flow on into the lives of those whom we need to forgive. We are commanded to "forgive as we have been forgiven" which is easy to say, but sometimes very, very hard to do.

A sure way of remaining in a dark and despairing place is to rehearse our hurts over and over. Just thinking about a person or situation that has contributed to our trauma can bring on agitation, a racing pulse, clammy hands, and tremors. As we replay how we've been used, abused, or abandoned, we dig a deeper and deeper rut into which our thoughts fall ever more easily. Rehearsing our hurts not only sends us further into darkness, but it also keeps us captive to bitterness and resentment.

Practicing forgiveness of others is the opposite of rehearsing our hurts. And practice is the key: we have all been seriously wounded by our abortion experiences and forgiving others takes time, determination, and repetition. Diligent effort strengthens our forgiveness muscles. With practice we can develop habits that will enhance all areas of our lives.

1. **Have you made a habit of rehearsing your hurts? Give several examples.**

2. **Make a list of ten words, or several phrases or statements, to describe the feeling of being completely forgiven by God. Refer back to the FEELINGS INVENTORY at the end of the first chapter if necessary.**

    Being completely forgiven by God makes me feel...

3. Now sit for several minutes with your eyes closed and think of the person connected to your abortion who has hurt you the most. Notice how your mind, body, and heart respond. Then complete the following:

    When I think about you, _____, *(insert that person's name) I feel...*

4. Compare your responses to the last two questions. How will passing along the forgiveness you have received affect your life?

5. Forgiving others does not mean that it is necessarily wise or safe to allow them back into our lives. Neither does our forgiveness let others off the hook for their offences. God will deal with them in due course. For now, sort those you need to forgive into two camps. Beside each name, list the reason(s) why you should or should not re-establish a relationship.

    • **After I have forgiven them, I might re-establish a relationship with the following:**

    • **After I have forgiven them, it would be unwise or unsafe to re-establish a relationship with the following:**

Dear friends, never avenge yourselves. Leave that to God. For it is written,
"I will take vengeance; I will repay those who deserve it," says the Lord.

Romans 12:19

BUT IT'S NOT FAIR!

You're absolutely right: the whole concept of forgiveness offends our human concept of justice and doesn't seem fair at all. But just as God disregards our human concept of justice by forgiving *us*, we are also required to override our concept of justice and forgive *others*.

1. **Look up "stew" in the dictionary. Record the definition that applies to an emotional state.**

2. **Describe ideas of revenge you have had towards those whom you now need to forgive. If you have acted on any of these ideas, record what you did here.**

3. **How have these thoughts or actions affected you? Did they assist your healing at all?**

4. **To help overcome our sense of injustice, it is tempting to make our forgiveness conditional. In other words, we're more willing to forgive a person who has had a change of heart or behavior. Complete the following sentences for those whom you need to forgive:**

    - **I may be able to forgive
      if only he/she/they would** _____

    - **I may be able to forgive
      if only he/she/they would** _____

    - **I may be able to forgive
      if only he/she/they would** _____

    - **I may be able to forgive
      if only he/she/they would** _____

5. **Did God establish any conditions in order for you to be forgiven? What does this tell you about the process of forgiving others? Do you think you can do it?**

6. **Complete the following statement over and over until you run out of ideas.**

Yes, I know forgiveness does not seem fair, but...

The bitterness of unforgiveness is like taking poison and waiting for the other person to die.
Henry Schorr

FORGIVENESS PIE

1.   **Make a list of the people you need to forgive:**

2.   **Now divide the pie into slices representing the amount of forgiveness each one requires from you.**

FORGIVENESS PIE

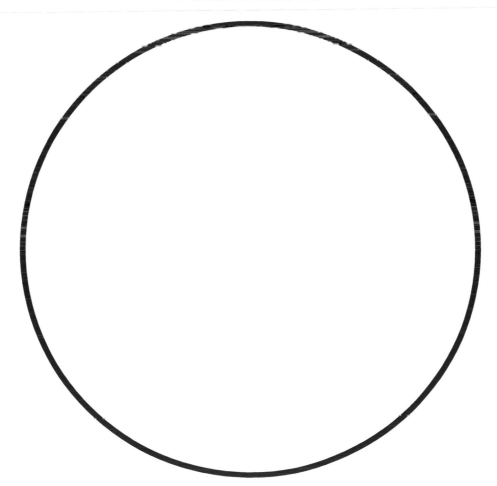

TRADING SHOES

"Walking a mile in their shoes" is a powerful technique that can help us forgive. By trying to imagine the pressures someone else faced because of our pregnancy and subsequent abortion, we can often find the compassion that was obscured by our own pain and stress.

This exercise is not intended to make excuses for evil. It is merely to assist you in forgiving from the heart. Here is your opportunity to trade shoes with those whom you need to forgive.

1. **Take the person, other than yourself, who needs your forgiveness the most and trade shoes for ten minutes. Try to imagine what was going through that person's mind and heart during the entire abortion experience. Now write a letter to yourself *from that person* explaining his/her side of the story.**

    Dear_____, (insert your own name)

2. **Using extra paper, continue writing short letters to yourself from the most significant people on your FORGIVENESS PIE.**

    Dear_____, (insert your own name)

3. **Do you think it will be easier to forgive now that you have completed this exercise?**

O Lord, you are so good, so ready to forgive, so full of unfailing love for all who ask for aid.

Psalm 86:5

FORGIVENESS CASE STUDY

After the shock of discovering her pregnancy, Veronica quickly became attached to her unborn child and named her "Sophie." She was excited and felt confident that she could depend on support from her boyfriend, Peter, as well as her close and loving family. Peter, however, was devastated and refused to allow Veronica to tell her family about the pregnancy.

Peter was determined that Veronica would have an abortion. When she resisted, he threatened to commit suicide. Eventually, buckling under the strain of Peter's relentless pleas and threats, Veronica submitted to abortion against her will.

Veronica worked steadily through her recovery program and thoroughly processed her anger and regret. After accepting God's forgiveness, she felt ready to extend forgiveness to Peter. Here is the letter she wrote and read aloud to her counselor. The writing alone achieved its purpose—the letter was never mailed.

Dear Peter,

Out of the forgiveness I have received from God, I forgive you for everything.

I forgive you for having unprotected sex ~ that's a two-way street ~ I can't place all of that responsibility on you.

I forgive you for using me. For wanting nothing more than just sex. It made me feel horrible. Used. Ugly. But I forgive you.

I forgive you for even placing the notion of abortion in my head. For making me even think that it was a good idea. For forcing me to make the biggest decision of my life.

I forgive you for manipulating me. For making me feel responsible for your life, as well as for Sophie's. You made me feel terrible...the worst I have ever felt. But I forgive you.

I forgive you for making me lie to my friends and family. For making me feel so desperate that I couldn't talk to the people who mean the most to me.

I forgive you for sobbing to me...for holding me when I was sobbing...because I knew it meant nothing. It was empty and all part of your grand scheme. But I forgive you.

I forgive you for abandoning me. I knew you had it planned out. I knew I wouldn't see you the same way after that Friday. And once you left, the realistic part of me knew it was done. That is when I needed somebody the most. I was so scared. But I forgive you for leaving.

I forgive you for not defending me when people thought I was crazy. Everybody thought I was foolish and desperate, and I felt stupid. I was. You didn't stop people from thinking that or dissuade them. But, I forgive you.

I forgive you for not recognizing important dates the way I wanted you to. I wanted you to ask me how I was, how I was coping, and if there was anything you could do. I just wanted you to validate my feelings. But you didn't. You played dumb. I forgive you for that.

I forgive you for not coming with me to counseling, or even making an effort. It made me feel so alone. Like I literally had nobody. You refused to help me. But I forgive you.

I forgive you for sleeping with Pamela, Taryn, and Diana. That made me feel used and like Sophie never existed for you. I was so angry. But I forgive you.

I forgive you for not loving me like I loved you. I just wanted us to be happy, even after Sophie's death. You couldn't do it. You couldn't even consider it. I was so hurt and disillusioned. But I forgive you.

I forgive you for stamping me out of your life. It hurts. Hurts that you won't even ask people how I am. That you wouldn't look at me during our last semester at school. I just wanted you to acknowledge my existence. But you didn't and you won't.

And I forgive you for that,

Veronica

PLEASE NOTE: This forgiveness letter, used by permission with changed names, illustrates how one young woman, with God's power, courageously confronted her own role and her partner's role in their abortion choice and its tragic aftermath. The forgiveness she experienced was life changing.

UPHILL TO FREEDOM

Writing sincere and effective forgiveness letters takes determination. If you are struggling, read aloud Henry Schorr's quote from a couple of pages back. Since this exercise is for your own healing, your letters are not intended to be sent. However, in some circumstances, after discussion with your counselor or mentor, it may be a valuable step to take.

You need to write a letter to each target on your Forgiveness Pie. If you become really angry as you think of a person, you must stop and write another anger letter before continuing. Your forgiveness letter will be a waste of time if you are still filled with anger or hatred towards the recipient.

Remember that forgiveness is a *decision*—not a *feeling*—and that it is *for your own benefit*. Ask God to guide your hand as you write.

1. **Make a few notes about how you feel before you start. If you feel agitated, you may want to breathe deeply, jog on the spot, or hum loudly.**

2. **Using extra paper, begin with a letter to God that focuses on *accepting* his forgiveness. This simple task will fill up your "forgiveness tank" so that you can then forgive the others on your pie.**

    Dear God,
    I _____ (insert your own name) accept your complete forgiveness for...

3. **Now take your forgiveness targets one by one and think over what you need to forgive them for. Use what you uncovered in the TRADING SHOES exercise if it is helpful. Include as much detail as necessary for each one.**

    Dear _____,
    Out of the forgiveness I have received from God, I forgive you for...

4. Reflect and record how you feel now that you have written your forgiveness letters, including how you feel physically.

5. What do you sense that God wants you to know about forgiveness?

6. After writing all your forgiveness letters, the most powerful thing to do is to read them aloud, preferably to a trusted person. Only after this is done will you decide what to do with them. You may need to keep them for a while and re-read them from time to time. Or you may choose to shred, burn, or bury them, or perhaps even throw them into the ocean. Write a short prayer that you might use as you dispose of your forgiveness letters.

7. Although you may have sincerely forgiven someone, you may eventually discover that bitterness and resentment have crept back into your soul. Refer back to PRACTICING FORGIVENESS, and then write and read aloud another forgiveness letter.

When you have a great and difficult task, something perhaps almost impossible,
if you work a little at a time, every day a little, suddenly the work will finish itself.

Isak Dinesen

IN THE SPOTLIGHT

If you have worked your way through these forgiveness exercises with an open, receptive, and willing heart, you are probably feeling significantly better. However, there is one more area that needs to be addressed before we move on.

In terms of becoming pregnant, it does "take two to tango." Some of us may have been pressured into sexual activity or even robbed of our innocence through abuse or rape. In most instances, however, we have been willing to participate with our partners. And, in the time before, during the abortion, and afterwards, we undoubtedly said or did things for which we are now sorry.

Psalm 51:10 says: *Create in me a clean heart, O God. Renew a right spirit within me.* Verse 17 continues with the observation: *The sacrifice you want is a broken spirit. A broken and repentant heart, O God, you will not despise.*

So now the spotlight is turned on us. It is time to search our own broken hearts for how we have wounded others on our sad journeys. It is time to take the steps that will release us from any lingering guilt and shame.

1. **Think back over your abortion experience and identify those whom you have wounded, whether they know it or not. For example, perhaps you chose abortion because you were too ashamed to seek the help of your parents. In doing so, you may have deprived them of much wanted grandchild. List those whose forgiveness you need to seek:**

2. **Sit quietly and think back to things you may have discovered in the TRADING SHOES exercise. Be courageous as you take ownership of your role in wounding others. Now take extra paper and write letters asking for the forgiveness of those you have hurt.**

    Dear_____,
        There are things that I have said or done that I deeply regret. Please forgive me for...

3. **What you do with these letters is entirely up to you. In some cases, composing a letter may inspire you to speak directly to the person and ask for their forgiveness. Or you may find it more appropriate to send your letter to the recipient.**

    In other situations, you may be unable to contact the recipient, or it may be unwise or dangerous to do so. If so, this may be an exercise that simply creates in you "a clean heart." After reading such a letter aloud, you may choose to either keep it or dispose of

it in due course. Discuss your letters with your counselor or mentor before taking further action.

4.   Try to find a picture that represents what the freedom of forgiveness feels like and paste it here. Add words if necessary.

You can't undo anything you've already done, but you can face up to it.
You can tell the truth. You can seek forgiveness.
And then let God do the rest.

Unknown

RELEASING OURSELVES

We often hear talk about the difficulty of "forgiving ourselves." But doing so is actually unnecessary because, when we ask, we are completely and utterly forgiven by God. When he forgives us it is a "done deal": there is no forgiving of ourselves to be done. What we do need to do, however, is get over our determination to punish ourselves.

God's forgiveness is really difficult to understand. It is all a function of "grace" or "undeserved favor." We tell ourselves that we *should* be punished; we *should* suffer terribly for what we have done. But we reckon this without God who, with all the authority of heaven, has paid the price for our sinfulness through the death of Jesus. He forgives us, setting us free to live lives of abundance and joy. Now all that is required is for us to release *ourselves* from the punishment we are convinced we deserve.

Consider this acronym for **GRACE**:

> **G**od's
> **R**ighteousness
> **A**t
> **C**hrist's
> **E**xpense

Yes, Christ has experienced intense suffering on our behalf, and we are now free. Our debt is paid in full.

In her novel *The Wonder Worker*, Susan Howatch emphasizes:

> *God's not interested in operating a brownie-point system ~ he's only interested in loving and forgiving those who are brave enough not to deny what they have done, no matter how terrible, brave enough to be truly sorry, brave enough to resolve to make a fresh start in serving him as well as they possibly can.*[11]

1. **Do you find it hard to imagine life lived in freedom, abundance and joy? Why?**

2. **Can you think of ways you have been punishing yourself?**

---

[11] Susan Howatch *The Wonder Worker* (New York: Fawcett Columbine/Ballantine Pub Group, 1998)

3.   Have you withheld pleasant experiences from yourself—nice clothes, a fun vacation, the time to sit and read a good book, etc.?

4.   Have you felt undeserving of a good relationship, a good job, a happy family, etc.? Explain how this sense of unworthiness has affected your life.

5.   Have you sabotaged opportunities because you felt undeserving? Describe.

6.   Think of as many things as you can that you have been withholding in order to punish yourself. Then make a collage entitled,

**I AM COMPLETELY FORGIVEN AND
GIVE MYSELF PERMISSION TO ENJOY...**

7.   Have you felt disqualified from certain opportunities to help or serve in your family, community, or church because of your abortion history? Do you feel differently now? What would you like to do?

*Justice is giving to others what they deserve.
Mercy is not giving what is deserved.
Grace is giving what is not deserved.*

Walt Larrimore

MY JOY LIST

Now that we have been forgiven and have released ourselves from condemnation, it is time to reconnect with joy. We may have developed a habit of denying ourselves joy, but this is about to change. On these pages, begin to create a list of seventy-five things that bring you joy. Add items to your Joy List as you discover them.

Use all your senses to experience joy: sight, sound, smell, taste, and touch. Here are a few examples to get you started: chocolate chip cookies, snow-covered spruce trees against a blue sky, the warmth of sunshine flowing through a window on a winter's day, the rich sound of a cello, multi-colored paperclips, a girls' night out, etc.

1.

2.

3.

4.

5.

6.

7.

8.

9.

10.

11.

12.

13.

14.

15.

16.

17.

18.

19.

20.

21.

22.

23.

24.

25.

26.

27.

28.

29.

30.

Joy is the serious business of heaven.

C. S. Lewis

CHAPTER SIX

HELLO THERE!

HELLO THERE!

In the normal course of living, it is most unusual to say "goodbye" to someone to whom we've never said "hello." Many of us have tried not to allow ourselves to think about our lost children, let alone say "hello," for fear that we will unleash a cascade of overwhelming grief.

However, getting to know our children, letting ourselves visualize them fully, and imagining what life might have been like with them allows us to dignify them with an identity. This process also allows us to recognize ourselves as mothers.

You will now have the opportunity to give your child the humanity that abortion denied. Don't be afraid of this process: you may find it to be surprisingly comforting. Hopefully, once you have completed this chapter, you will find it much easier to imagine your child safe in heaven with Jesus.

So far you have dealt with much of the toxic emotional fallout from your abortion. Now it is time to begin the next part of your journey, focusing on what you have lost. Once you have recognized and named your losses, you will be able to grieve and heal.

OPPORTUNITY KNOCKS

Abortion results in loss—very real, gut-wrenching loss—and grieving our lost children is what this program is all about. However, our children are not necessarily our only losses: other losses ushered in by abortion need to be identified and grieved as well.

Although by now we have asked for, and received, complete forgiveness for our *actions*, the *consequences* of our choices may still be causing us pain. Yet these difficult consequences related to our abortions do not disqualify us from having a satisfying and joyful future. Our losses simply need to be confronted and dealt with in life-affirming ways. Then, with courage and creativity, we can find ways to say "hello" to new opportunities.

1. **Highlight any of the following losses that also occurred when you chose abortion:**

    - **My physical health**

    - **My reproductive health**

    - **My self-esteem**

    - **My innocence**

    - **My relationship with my partner:** _____

    - **My relationship with the following family members:** _____

    _____

    - **My relationship with these friends:** _____

    _____

    - **My relationship with God**

    - **My hopes and dreams of marriage**

    - **My hopes and dreams of motherhood**

    - **Other:** _____

    _____

2. **These losses may cause you deep disappointment and sadness, but there is usually *something* that you can do to improve the situation.**

    Follow the four-part format in the following example to process your three most serious losses (or more, if you have time). Start by naming the loss. Then write a reflection on how your life has been impacted. Think creatively about how you could turn this loss around and say "hello" to opportunity. Finish with a solid action step.

Loss: *Hopes and dreams of motherhood*

Reflection: *As a little girl I always dreamed of having a large family. I spent many happy hours considering names and trying to decide how many boys and how any girls I would like. These ideas changed almost daily. After my abortion I sabotaged relationship after relationship and turned instead to my career, a career that would continue to be a steady part of my life.*

Before I knew it, the years had flown by. I entered menopause a couple of years ago and the end of my childbearing years. I was devastated and continue to be haunted by the knowledge that I will never spend time cuddling my own babies or grandbabies. There is an ache in my heart that won't go away.

Hello to Opportunity: *I have recently heard about a program at our local hospital that needs volunteers to cuddle babies whose moms are unavailable.*

Action Step: *Tomorrow I will call the hospital and find out what I need to do to become a baby cuddler.*

Begin processing your most hurtful loss below. Then continue on, using extra paper.

REPLACEMENT BABY

When something is broken or lost, our natural reaction is to replace it. The toaster gives up, so out it goes and a new one takes its place. Even living things such as a dog or cat will often be "replaced" when they die. However, we know that unlike a toaster, we can never really replace a beloved pet—a living creature. No other pet could ever have the same character or replicate the uniqueness of the prior relationship.

When we lose a child to abortion, adoption, miscarriage, accident, or disease we are left with an aching void that must be faced. If our grief work is not done thoroughly, the unresolved pain tempts us to fill that void by trying to replace the loss with another child.

This desire can take on a life of its own. Women who have had abortions sometimes endanger themselves by returning to abusive partners in order to try to redo the pregnancy, with the same father, and thereby replace the baby. It is an empty victory, however, as no other child can possibly replace the unique baby lost to abortion.

If another baby *is* conceived and delivered as a replacement, that child is charged with a suffocating responsibility. It is quite enough for a child to live up to parental expectations, without the additional burden of compensating for their unresolved abortion issues. It goes without saying that these pressures are grossly unfair, and that eventual rebellion by the child is practically guaranteed.

1. **Have you had thoughts of trying to become pregnant again? Did those thoughts haunt you over and over?**

2. **Have you tried to become pregnant? Perhaps with the same man?**

3. **What do you think you would achieve by having a "do-over"?**

4. **Knowing the dangers of trying to replace your baby, write a warning statement to yourself to remember when those thoughts occur. Or, if you have succeeded in delivering a replacement baby, write a warning statement to yourself about the importance of grieving well so that your child is not burdened with unrealistic expectations.**

GRIEVING 101

Some cultures have clearly defined rituals for grieving the losses that inevitably occur. Other cultures shrink from grief, trying to out-maneuver the pain. Western cultures in particular are notorious for using busyness to ward off grief. However, sorrow must always accompany loss, so we might as well learn how to deal with it in ways that bring healing to ourselves and to our loved ones.

Ungrieved losses take a heavy toll on our hearts. Imagine your loss as a pile of rocks pressing down on your heart, crushing the life out of it. It's no wonder we feel deadened emotionally while bearing the weight of a loss that has yet to be fully relinquished.

By now you have made a great deal of progress in your grieving journey. You have removed many of the rocks of denial, anger, shame, guilt, and unforgiveness. However, further rocks representing the barrier between yourself and your child still need to be removed. With each stone lifted, you will feel the pressure lightening and your heart coming back to life.

1. **How did your family of origin handle loss? What did you learn about grieving as you grew up?**

2. **Have you observed others doing their grieving well? What was it about the process that made it memorable?**

3. **Have you felt comforted by the presence of others on your grieving journey? Who are they, and how have they helped?**

4. **What do you wish you had known about grieving?**

5. **Do you feel better equipped now?**

6. How will you behave differently when you are confronted with another loss?

7. Give three words or phrases to describe the difference when the pressure of a deadening burden is removed from your heart.

We must empty ourselves of grief to make room for grace and forgiveness.

Theresa Burke

GETTING TO KNOW YOU

Allowing ourselves the privilege of getting to know our children can be very healing. We don't do this to dwell on our children forever. Rather, we get to "know" them in order to grieve the loss of them. Once we have worked through our grief, we can say "goodbye for now," confident that we will meet again in heaven.

Don't hesitate to ask God to direct you through this process. One woman, during this stage of her journey, was struggling to imagine her child. Trudy thought it might have been a girl, but felt swayed by the fact that a girl is what she would have wanted. Her thoughts felt flimsy and unconvincing, and she experienced no peace. Her counselor suggested that Trudy ask God to reveal her child to her if it would help her heal.

This is what Trudy said to her counselor when she returned the following week:

It felt a bit weird to do this, but I did pray and ask God to reveal my child to me. Not only did he reveal that my child is a boy, but also that his name is Thomas.

1. **Have you had any dreams or visions of your child? Describe what you saw and felt.**

2. **Do you have a strong sense of whether your child was a boy or girl?**

3. **Have you named your child? Why did you choose this particular name?**

4. **Did you let yourself imagine your baby when you were pregnant? Did you talk to him or her? What did you say?**

5. **When you imagine your child now, at what age or stage is he or she?**

6.   What do you think that your child would look like? Why?

7.   Can you imagine what kind of personality your child might have had?

8.   Might your child have had certain natural abilities or talents? Why?

9.   What kinds of activities would you have enjoyed doing together?

10.   Are there special family traditions that your child would have grown up with?

11.   What special things can you do that you would have loved to teach your child?

FACE TO FACE

Visualizing our children in heaven is comforting. For our peace of mind, however, we need to be absolutely certain that this is where they are. Thankfully, God's Word provides us with the assurance we need.

1. **Consider the following verses from Psalm 139:13-16a. Then record when your unborn baby's life began.**

    You made all the delicate, inner parts of my body and knit me together in my mother's womb. Thank you for making me so wonderfully complex! Your workmanship is marvelous ~ how well I know it. You watched me as I was being formed in utter seclusion, as I was woven together in the dark of the womb. You saw me before I was born.

2. **Read about the death of King David's son, found in 2 Samuel 12:19-23.**

    When David saw them whispering, he realized what had happened. "Is the child dead?" he asked. "Yes," they replied, "he is dead."

    Then David got up from the ground, washed himself, put on lotions, and changed his clothes. He went to the Tabernacle and worshiped the Lord. After that, he returned to the palace and was served food and ate. His advisers were amazed. "We don't understand you," they told him. "While the child was still living, you wept and refused to eat. But now that the child is dead, you have stopped your mourning and are eating again."

    David replied, "I fasted and wept while the child was alive, for I said, 'Perhaps the Lord will be gracious to me and let the child live.' But why should I fast when he is dead? Can I bring him back again? I will go to him one day, but he cannot return to me."

3. **Which statement in this passage gives you assurance that your child is in heaven?**

4. **What do you imagine heaven to be like for your child?**

5. **How will you feel seeing your child face to face?**

6.   What is the first thing you want to do when you see your child in heaven?

7.   What do you want to say to your child?

8.   What do you imagine being with Jesus is like for your child?

9.   Besides being with Jesus, do you imagine your child in the company of other loved ones who have died? Who are they?

10.   Since I have given my child a name and identity and can now imagine him or her in heaven, I feel...

But Jesus said, "Let the children come to me. Don't stop them!
For the Kingdom of Heaven belongs to such as these."

Matthew 19:14

HANGING OUT

Now that you have allowed yourself to name and visualize your child, you have a focus for your grief. It is hard to mourn the loss of a person you don't know in some way, so this is your opportunity to get to know your child by spending some time together.

Some people engage with their emotions very naturally through words and writing. As they pick up a pen, the words just seem to pour out of them easily and effectively. Others are more visual and find pictures easier to relate to, whether the images are on paper or in the imagination. For this exercise you can choose to write, or create a collage, or a combination of both.

Give yourself plenty of time to do this project: to be effective, it must not be rushed. Remember that you are getting to know your child, so honor him or her with your time and effort.

1. **Write a lengthy reflection or create a comprehensive collage to represent at least one of the following. Use as much detail as possible.**

    *   **A day spent together with your child, at any age you choose, doing exactly what you wish you could have done together.**

    *   **A special time such as Christmas, summer vacation, Easter, extended family get-together, backyard barbeque with family friends, etc.**

    *   **Your child's growing up years from birth to adulthood. Include activities and milestones.**

2. **Once you have completed this project, describe how you feel about "knowing" your child more intimately.**

LETTER TO BEN

Dear Ben,

It is snowing today and I'm thinking of you...

It was so ugly before the snow came, the garden dead, the trees mostly bare. Every year I have to convince myself that the beauty and life of summer are just rolled up for storage ~ they haven't gone, never to return.

But then the snow comes and a blanket of white gently covers the ugliness of dirt and debris beneath. Much like the way Jesus has covered my own sins and scars: the way he has made me into a new creation, gently cloaking me with his forgiveness and mercy. But though there is forgiveness, I still have to live with the consequences of my sin, and so do you, my beloved little boy.

You would have loved the snow. Your Dad was a competitive skier and really wanted me to get involved, but my southern blood cringed at the thought of all that cold, back then. What a joke ~ to think that I have lived with at least six months of winter each year ever since! He would have been a good teacher, a good Dad, because his Dad ~ your Grandpa ~ was such a wonderful father. He would have loved to teach you all about fishing as well. There would have certainly been saltwater in your blood, Ben, what with a Dad who grew up on boats, and a Mom who was always in and out of the ocean as well.

Ben, the pain of not seeing you grow up to be the big brother of my other children is so very, very hard. In fact, for years I didn't let myself think about you very much because it made me so sad. But it doesn't mean that I love you less.

At least I know what you looked like as a little boy. God, in his grace, gave me a vision of you running towards me and flinging yourself into my arms. You wrapped your little arms around my neck and hugged me so close. I could even smell the little boy smell of you and feel your silky hair against my cheek. What a gift that continues to be to me.

I wish I could feel your hugs again and that I could celebrate with you the courage I had to carry you to term. But we know that my decision instead was one of panic, cowardice, and shame. So now we pay the price of being separated by a distance that can only be closed by imagination and prayer.

Ben, next spring you would have celebrated your 25th birthday. I know you would have been tall and slim like your Dad; that you would have been athletic and had many fun times with your brothers, who would have looked up to you as the oldest of the clan.

I'm sure we wouldn't have escaped without broken windows and broken bones, the odd banged up car, and other casualties due to the rumblings of testosterone. But what a journey we would have made: your first tooth and your first day at school, your first date and graduation day, your coming to faith then maybe questioning what it is all about, your choice of career, and your choice of a wife.

Ben, what your life would have been will be a mystery to me forever. It is a loss that I chose when I wrote a cheque for $100 and submitted to the procedure that would tear us apart for my lifetime.

Yet God, in his mercy, has used this shattering loss to bring me into his kingdom and transform my life. God's word promises that we will be reunited in heaven. I am just so very sorry that you have been lost to me for all these intervening years.

I love you so,

      Mom

PLEASE NOTE: This letter is used by permission of its author.

1. **After reading this mother's letter to her son, sit quietly and try to imagine what *you* would like to say to *your* child. Use this time to review your experience. Think and feel deeply about the personhood of your child, and let yourself explore how he or she would have fitted into your life and activities. When you are ready, take extra paper and write your letter by hand.**

2. **Now that you have poured out your heart to your child, it's time to allow your child to respond to you. Take a few deep breaths and, when you feel calm and ready, welcome your child into your heart and mind. Take some more paper if necessary and record, in letter form, what you sense *your child* would like to say to *you*.**

To send a letter is a good way to go somewhere without moving anything but your heart.

      Phyllis Theroux

CHAPTER SEVEN

GOODBYE FOR NOW

GOODBYE FOR NOW

Bringing closure to our grief journey can be difficult. Although it is a relief to say goodbye to toxic emotions such as anger, guilt, and pain, it is much, much harder to say goodbye to our children. Many of us have only just allowed ourselves to know them for the first time—and now we have to let them go?

Yes, we do. Unless we release our children into God's care, we will continue to be stuck in a cycle of unfinished grief. Our children deserve the peace of being at home in heaven, and we need the peace of knowing they are there.

We have explored our experiences and the impact upon our lives from many different angles. We have told and retold our stories. As we have done these things, we have developed a shape and rhythm to our sad sagas. We now have a beginning, middle, and end to our abortion loss and can place it in the context of our lives. Our abortions do not define who we are: they are simply a tragic loss encountered along life's journey.

Now that we have dignified our children by allowing ourselves to name them and know them, it's time to release them to heaven where there are no more tears, no more weeping. It's time to say "goodbye for now."

MY, HOW YOU'VE GROWN!

How easy it is to fall into the trap of dwelling on the "if onlys" of our lives! Saying "if only" is as helpful as stepping hard on the accelerator and brake pedals at the same time. We make a lot of noise and smoke, waste gasoline, and ruin our brake pads—while getting absolutely nowhere. Although regret is natural after abortion, it must not be allowed to rob us of joy.

Keep in mind that our suffering will not be wasted. As Romans 5:3-4 says,

> *We can rejoice, too, when we run into problems and trials, for we know that they are good for us ~ they help us to learn to endure. And endurance develops strength of character in us, and character strengthens our confident expectation of salvation.*

Once we have confronted our mistakes and received forgiveness, we must put the past into the past where it belongs. It is time to say goodbye to regret and remorse over our abortions, once and for all.

You may have tormented yourself with all kinds of "if onlys" before this healing journey. Are there any that are *still* bothering you? If so, complete the three steps below before moving on to question four.

1.   **First, record each "if only" that lingers.**

     •   **If only...**

     •   **If only...**

     •   **If only...**

2.   **Now, go back to the first chapter of this book and read CHOOSE YOUR BELIEFS CARE-FULLY again. Are you choosing to believe lies about the effectiveness of your healing?**

3. Take each leftover "if only." Respond to it by examining the good that has come from your painful situation or decision. Use the example below for ideas.

    If only I hadn't become involved with Mark and hadn't let him talk me into having sex...but I did, and the outcome was a terrible disaster. However, if this hadn't happened, I would never have understood how to grieve well and experience health and joy again. I have learned so much. Now I know that I don't have to settle for a rotten relationship. I'm going to focus on being healthy in every area of my life, starting with never letting "if onlys" torment me again!!

4. Consider the verses from Romans on the prior page. Then reflect on your abortion and healing experience.

    - **The main problems and trials I faced because of my abortion were...**

    - **The good that came out of them was...**

    - **My endurance has developed in the following way(s)...**

    - **The changes to my strength of character include...**

    - **The hope I have for the future is...**

5. Write a statement that summarizes how your abortion trauma and healing have caused you to grow.

Adversity precedes growth.

Rosemarie Rossetti

MISSING MOTHERHOOD

Some of us have been fortunate enough to have children besides those we have lost to abortion. Others have not. Perhaps you haven't met the right man. Maybe another pregnancy seems to be eluding you. Or the arrival of menopause has put an end to hopes and dreams of a baby. If so, this exercise is for you, in particular...

And it is also for all of us, women who will never mother, in this lifetime, the unique children lost to us.

1.   **What is the most significant thing you regret about not mothering your unborn child?**

2.   **As you think about your lost opportunity, take another sheet of paper and pour out your agony and disappointment to God. Then listen for anything he may be telling you, and record it here.**

3.   **Which parts of mothering would you have looked forward to?**

4.   **Which parts of mothering would you have been anxious about?**

5. How were you mothered? Would you want to mother your own child the same way, or in another way?

6. When you think of a great mom, who comes to mind? Why?

7. If you can't deliver and raise your own naturally born child, would you rather have no child at all? If you feel this way, could you now consider some other approach to investing in babies or children?

8. Do you have a close relationship with children in your extended family or those belonging to your friends? What do you like to do with them?

9. Have you ever considered adopting or fostering a child? What went through your mind and heart as you thought about this?

10. Are there young moms in your neighborhood who would love to have you invest time and interest in their children?

11. Make a list of ways you could develop relationships with children: volunteering at a local school, teaching Sunday School, coaching a team, mentoring, becoming a "Big Sister" to an at-risk child, etc. Explore your areas of interest for ideas.

12. Record an action step for becoming more involved with a child or children, when you are ready to do so.

MEMORIALIZATION

Many people have discovered that the act of selecting a meaningful memorial can offer healing and bring closure to a loss. Just contemplating what the memorial might be is helpful, as it honors the reality and memory of our children and brings dignity to their shortened lives. Consider the following ideas, but don't let them stifle your own heart's leading:

- Plant a tree or dedicate a garden to your child's memory. You may also include your child's name on a plaque and mount it on a garden bench.

- Write a poem or song, paint a picture, or make a quilt.

- Have a private candlelight memorial service for your child.

- Choose a memory box for your child to hold significant items.

- Create a special collection of songs that remind you of the love you have for your child. You may like to write a letter or poem to your child and include it as an introduction to your collection.

- Donate books on infant loss and grief to your local library or support groups in your child's name.

- At Christmas, purchase or make an ornament that symbolizes your child at the age he or she would be now. For example, select a school-themed ornament for a six-year-old, or a key ornament for a teen of driving age.

- Select a piece of jewellery that commemorates your child.

- Find a figurine or other piece of art that depicts your love for your child.

- Buy yourself a Bible or another meaningful book that will serve as a connection between you and your child.

- Build a cairn (a pile of stones used, in ancient times, as a tribute to loved ones who have been lost).

- Select a children's book that you would have loved to read with your child.

- Find a piece of literature or scripture that speaks to your heart and have it mounted and framed.

- Do something physical in honour of your child's memory, such as running a half-marathon, climbing a mountain, or hiking to a significant destination.

- Perform a ritual such as going to the beach, sitting quietly to contemplate your child, and then drawing something meaningful in the sand. Sit and wait until the tide comes in to wash it away, along with your grief.

- A wonderful act of love is charity. Donate to a cause that touches your heart in honour of your child. Or sponsor a child the same age as yours would have been. Try it once—the feeling is wonderful!

1.   These are just a few of the endless memorialization possibilities available to you. Read them over and see whether one seems like a good fit for you. Record it here, along with the steps you need to take to carry it out.

2.   Alternatively, develop your own memorial activity and describe it here, including the steps to carry it out.

CALEB'S MEMORIAL SERVICE

This account is just one highly personal way to conduct a memorial service. You may be inspired to plan your own service, or may pick out ideas for your own use. There are countless ways to honor your child; a memorial service is just one of them.

I had a little service last Friday evening for Caleb. My pastor helped us out and we held the service in a prayer chapel where we wouldn't be disturbed. There was such a reverent feeling in there.

My adult son, Josh, brought along some close friends. And my friend, Phil, also wanted to attend. He had fathered an unborn child about twenty years ago, and he has grieved that loss over the years. So I was supported by five, big, strong guys. They're all jocks, but very caring ~ even jocks can shed a tear!

The pastor spoke at the beginning of the service after a song was played. Josh and I both spoke some words for Caleb, and Josh played a song he wrote for the occasion on his cello. We had candles and a few special songs on the CD player.

Josh brought along some special objects that signify important aspects for him. These included a story and a sword. He read out of the Bible about the special bond between Joshua and Caleb, and said that he will meet his brother in the Promised Land that lies ahead.

It was really something to see Josh's friends supporting him. Big jocks can have big hearts... they actually asked to come! It's not the kind of event that a lot of people (maybe especially men) would want to attend or would even understand. Also, my sister, who lives overseas, sent a beautiful bouquet of flowers for us to have there.

Having this service has really made a difference for me in my healing; it provided a way for me to say I am sorry and be respectful in a concrete way. However, the main purpose was to honor and respect Caleb, which is what I feel we accomplished. It was certainly a tribute to Caleb, and the prayers and words spoken were all about honoring him.

It was so special...

PLEASE NOTE: this account is used by permission of its author with key names unchanged.

ABORTION WOUND REVISITED

Reflecting upon how an abortion wound has changed can be a helpful indication of healing. A wound once imagined as a pile of rubble and debris, for example, might become transformed into a garden of tiny flowers pushing their way through the wreckage.

The woman whose abortion wound felt like shattered glass (described in MY ABORTION WOUND, chapter one) experienced a dramatic transformation. After her healing journey, she realized that there *had been* one person who was willing to gather up the broken glass, and in doing so, bleed on her behalf. That person was Jesus. With his wounded hands, he had gathered and melted down the shards, created a beautiful pitcher, and filled it to the brim with his living water. Now he was using that pitcher to pour living water into the lives of other women broken by abortion.

Look up the description of your own abortion wound in the first chapter. Reflect upon what you were trying to express back then. Now take several minutes to consider how your healing journey has affected your wound.

1.   **Has your abortion wound changed?**

2.   **If so, describe how it has changed. What does it look like or feel like now?**

3.   **Are you surprised by what has happened? Explain.**

4.   **What does this transformation tell you about your healing journey?**

MEMORY BOX

1. Take your time assembling the following items, and choose a suitable box in which to keep them:

   • A card welcoming a new baby.

   • A poem, quote, or scripture verse that you would choose to include in a baptism or baby dedication service. Record these words here as well.

   • An item or small piece of clothing for your baby. Describe.

   • A sympathy card for a baby who has died.

   • A poem, quote, or scripture verse that you would choose to Include in a memorial service for your baby. Record these words here as well.

   • A memorial token for your baby. Describe what it is, and why you chose it.

2. What do you notice about the nature of the items above? What about the order in which they are listed? What inescapable reality must you now face?

JOURNEY ALPHABET

It is important to be spontaneous for this exercise. Find a word, words, or a phrase related to your healing journey that starts with each letter:

A _____

B _____

C _____

D _____

E _____

F _____

G _____

H _____

I _____

J _____

K _____

L _____

M _____

N _____

O _____

P _____

Q _____

R _____

S _____

T _____

U _____

V _____

W _____

X _____

Y _____

Z _____

1.   Look for patterns in your choice of words or statements. Do most of them have a positive or negative flavor? Do your words indicate a healing trend? A transformation?

2.   What did you learn from reviewing your journey in this way?

3.   Are there areas that still need work? If so, note them here.

4.   Who will hold you accountable for getting that work done?

5.   Refer back to the first chapter of this book. Read your answers for the CONFRONTING THE CHALLENGE exercise. Was that preparation helpful for what you actually experienced on your journey? Is there anything you wish you had been warned about at the outset?

6.   Do your answers show strength, self-understanding, growth, new skills, or a deeper faith? Record what you have gained.

BALLOON CEREMONY

You may have already decided to have a memorial service for your child, but even if you have, a balloon ceremony, or a ritual like it, will be valuable. Balloons are a familiar part of significant rites of passage—births, birthdays, or milestones. Since children, in particular, take a simple delight in them, it seems appropriate to use balloons for this significant milestone in our healing journey.

Watching a helium-filled balloon sail away into the sky can bring mixed feelings. While the one who releases it suffers a loss, the balloon, free at last, soars to great heights. All of the things we have been having difficulty releasing are symbolically set free as well, allowed to sail away to God, once and for all.

There is some reflection needed in preparation for this ceremony. You have already released a great deal of pain as you have worked through this program. However, there may still be a few leftover pieces that need to be released. Take your time and use this opportunity to bring closure to your abortion experience.

1.   **Name any *leftover* toxic emotions that you need to release.**

2.   **Name any *leftover* remorse or regrets that you need to release.**

3.   **Name any unhealthy involvements that you need to be rid of.**

4.   **Name any relationships (besides the one that you have with your child) that you need to say goodbye to.**

5. On a separate piece of paper, write a statement that frees you from the items and people identified in the first four questions. Read your statement aloud, and ask God to make this a reality in your life as you dispose of your note.

6. Name your child. Then list what you have lost as mother of this child, specific opportunities that you need to say goodbye to:

7. Compose a statement or prayer that releases the things you have named in the question above. Finish with a closing farewell to your child as you commit him or her to God. Copy it onto a very small piece of paper.

BALLOON CEREMONY

Purchase a helium-filled balloon in a suitable color.
If you are traveling to the location of your ceremony,
bring along a spare balloon in case of a mishap!

Choose a wide open, meaningful place for your balloon ceremony,
somewhere beautiful and peaceful.

Spend some time reflecting and praying for the strength you need
to say goodbye. Ask God to use this ceremony to bring
your grieving journey to a close.

Read what you have written aloud, and then tie
your piece of paper to the string of your balloon.

When you are ready,
release your balloon and say goodbye...

CHAPTER EIGHT

LIVING IN COLOR

LIVING IN COLOR

These days, in our culture, it is almost fashionable to be constantly "in therapy." In her book *A Crisis of Care*, Patricia Benner notes: *We have made recovery a never-ending project instead of an epiphany, a new beginning.* But this need not be the case.

After all the hard work of grieving and healing, a new beginning is precisely what we can expect. M. Craig Barnes describes this hope in his book *When God Interrupts*:

> They thought their cancer or their divorce or their grief meant the end of their lives. They were right. Life as they knew it was over. In its place they were given not just a new life, but a new purpose to life.

Over and over women describe feeling as though they themselves died on that terrible day of their abortion. Certainly some of us feel that we *deserved* to die for our choices. But, as Barnes points out, although something *did* come to an end, and life as we knew it *is* over, a new life and purpose have taken its place. Living in the grey zone is now a thing of the past: living in color is our new reality.

The intense work of your grief journey has now come to an end. It may take some time to feel the complete effect of your healing and to fully experience your new capacity for joy, but please don't doubt that your healing has been profound. Look back at how far you have come, and be patient and confident that God will use this experience, and your healing, powerfully in your life.

So what now? Transformed by recovery and armed with tools for healthy living, it is time to embrace a life of vibrant color—one of hope, purpose, and joy. So let's explore what the new you has to offer the world.

He has given me a new song to sing, a hymn of praise to our God.
Many will see what he has done and be astounded.
They will put their trust in the Lord.

Psalm 40:3

MANASSEH'S RESTORATION STORY

If you ever doubted that God has the desire and power to rescue and restore those who do evil, doubt no more! This life-changing story from the Bible has been recorded for the benefit of all generations. Manasseh's remarkable restoration is especially powerful for those of us who have had abortions.

Manasseh was twelve years old when he became king, and he reigned in Jerusalem fifty-five years. He did what was evil in the Lord's sight, following the detestable practices of the pagan nations that the Lord had driven from the land ahead of the Israelites. He rebuilt the pagan shrines his father, King Hezekiah, had broken down. He constructed altars and set up Asherah poles for pagan worship. He also bowed before all the powers of the heavens (other than God) and worshiped them.

He built pagan altars in the Temple of the Lord, the place where the Lord had said, "My name will remain in Jerusalem forever." Manasseh also sacrificed his own sons in the fire in the valley of Ben-Hinnom. He practiced sorcery, divination, and witchcraft, and he consulted with mediums and psychics. He did much that was evil in the Lord's sight, arousing his anger. Manasseh also murdered many innocent people until Jerusalem was filled from one end to the other with innocent blood. He led the people of Judah and Jerusalem to do even more evil than the pagan nations that the Lord had destroyed when the people of Israel entered the land.

The Lord spoke to Manasseh and his people, but they ignored all his warnings. So the Lord sent the commanders of the Assyrian armies, and they took Manasseh prisoner. They put a ring through his nose, bound him in bronze chains, and led him away to Babylon. But while in deep distress, Manasseh cried out to the Lord his God and sincerely humbled himself before the God of his ancestors. And when he prayed, the Lord listened to him and was moved by his request. So the Lord brought Manasseh back to Jerusalem and to his kingdom. Then Manasseh finally realized that the Lord alone is God!

After this, Manasseh rebuilt the outer wall of the City of David. He built the wall very high. And he stationed his military officers in all of the fortified towns of Judah. Manasseh also removed the foreign gods and the idol from the Lord's Temple. He tore down all the altars he had built on the hill where the Temple stood and all the altars that were in Jerusalem, and he dumped them outside the city. Then he restored the altar of the Lord and sacrificed peace offerings and thanksgiving offerings on it. He also encouraged the people of Judah to worship the Lord, the God of Israel.

When Manasseh died, he was buried in his palace. Then his son Amon became the next king.

Condensation of 2 Chronicles 33:1-20 and 2 Kings 21:16

1. Find three pens of different colors.

    • Use one to underline everything that Manasseh did that was *sinful* in the eyes of God.

    • Use another color to underline each action by the Lord God.

    • Use the third color to underline everything that Manasseh did that was *pleasing* to God.

2. How would you describe Manasseh's character and leadership?

3. What exactly did Manasseh do that finally changed the course of his life?

4. How did God respond? Note each undeserved blessing Manasseh received.

5. What do you find surprising in this story?

6. Do you find this story comforting? If so, explain exactly why you do.

7.   Doubts about your healing and restoration will almost certainly surface from time to time. This insecurity tends to manifest itself during periods of spiritual distance from God. Focused prayer should be your first line of defense. And, at such times, other creative tips can be used to bring the powerful message of this story back to mind. Add to the example given.

    a)   Write "Manasseh" on your bathroom mirror with an erasable marker, or on a note taped inside your bathroom cabinet.

    b)

    c)

THE TURRET

Do you find it hard to focus on the present or to look forward to the future? Is it more instinctive to turn and stare back into the past? Although we cannot physically go back in time, we can certainly go backwards mentally, emotionally, or spiritually—often to our detriment.

A common expression in our culture is to "move on," usually in reference to being "over" a situation or relationship. However, looking forward and moving on after completing a post-abortion recovery journey isn't so simple: it takes both strength of purpose and an unshakeable confidence in our healing.

If you find yourself fluctuating between freedom and despair from time to time, please don't allow it to undermine your healing. Simply return to the page of forgiveness verses in the FINDING WINGS chapter. Read them over and over while asking God to fix the truth of his words in your heart. Refresh the memorization of your favorite verse and repeat it to yourself.

Recognize that negative thinking is not from God. James 1:6b warns that *a doubtful mind is as unsettled as a wave of the sea that is driven and tossed by the wind*. The last thing that God would want is for any doubt to creep into your heart and take your focus off of his power to forgive and restore you for all eternity.

Now, sit comfortably and allow your imagination to take over as you contemplate the following story adapted from Anthony de Mello's *The Heart of the Enlightened*.

Imagine that you are climbing upwards in a tower. As you climb, are you constantly looking over your shoulder, or are you looking ahead in eager anticipation of what you will find? Now imagine that you are overcome by a strange feeling and, as you glance backwards, you see that each step you have climbed has dropped away into thin air...

1. **Take plenty of time to imagine yourself in this story. Pay close attention to any physical sensations you are experiencing. How does it feel to apply this concept to your life today?**

2. **God's love for us is unimaginable. His desire to rescue us from the deepest depths of darkness, as in Manasseh's story, can be proven true in our own lives as well. Did your abortion cause you to lose sight of what a vibrant, joy-filled life was, or might be, like?**

3. Now that you have experienced the power of God to forgive you, and have learned of his desire to restore you, do you have a different attitude towards your future? Describe.

4. Describe at least one action step to activate what you are looking forward to in each of these areas:

    •   **Your personal life**

    •   **Your spiritual life**

    •   **Your relationships**

    •   **Your career, education, or other pursuit**

5. Choose a word or phrase that you can use to remind yourself of the need to keep climbing upwards.

WHAT ABOUT TELLING OTHERS?

The thought of telling others about our abortions usually fills us with dread. Even after a life-changing recovery, it is nerve-wracking to imagine introducing such a controversial topic into a conversation. Even more worrisome are the reactions we might receive.

Do not believe for a minute that your unwillingness to tell others about your abortion means that you have not healed properly. God alone knows when, and if, it is necessary to disclose this very private matter. He alone will make it abundantly clear when you are to say anything.

Secrets throw up barriers between people. The closer the relationship is, the more important it is to maintain a healthy transparency. The saying, "the healthiest family is the one with the fewest secrets," is true. Telling immediate family about our abortion losses *may* be a healthy thing to do, though timing is crucial and details are not necessary.

Over and over again we encounter post-abortive women who are horrified by the prospect of telling anyone outside their counseling or recovery groups. However, as time passes and their healing becomes more secure, many develop a distinct restlessness and realize that God is preparing them to disclose to certain people. Praying for confirmation and courage, and then stepping out in obedience, are the next steps.

There are various reasons why it may be necessary or helpful to disclose your abortion:

- When a dating relationship becomes serious and is heading for marriage, it is only fair to disclose this part of your history to the man with whom you are planning to spend the rest of your life.

- Whereas the keeping of this secret creates a barrier to true intimacy within a marriage, or between close friends or family members, disclosure can create a bridge.

- Children seem to have a sixth sense about abortion. Although they have no idea why, they often feel a sense of loss, or a sense that something vital is missing. They may even experience "survivor guilt": a haunting sense that they don't deserve to be alive when someone else is not. Telling our children, and addressing their questions and concerns in an age-appropriate way, can be a huge relief for both parties.

- If one parent, brother, or sister knows, and others don't, a burden of secrecy is often placed upon that person. He or she may be constantly on guard during family interactions, fearing the damage an accidental comment could inflict. The pressure to protect you, combined with the longing to be transparent with other family members, can place your confidante in an unsettling position. However, on the other hand, there may be compelling reasons why telling certain family members is not wise.

- Professionals you consult about your physical, emotional, or spiritual health will better understand your case if you disclose.

- God may want you to make a connection with someone who needs to be led to a healing opportunity. Or, by speaking up, you may prevent another woman from making the decision to abort without fully understanding the consequences.

Disclosure needs to be handled with patience and faith. You can never control the ability of another to protect your privacy. Take time to pray for guidance, wait for clear confirmation, and disclose with great care.

TELLING OTHERS CASE STUDY

My heart races as I push the send button on the e-mail I just spent hours composing... God forgives our every sin. But in his great love, he does not remove the consequences of our choices...

The Lord had laid it on my heart to tell my two grown boys about the older sister they were never allowed to have. Their father and I had chosen abortion for their sister so we could finish our college degrees. (We divorced several years ago.) I struggled with the decision to tell my sons. My prayers were many, mostly asking the Lord to relieve me from this task.

Pushing the button to send that e-mail brings a thousand fears to mind. Will he hate me? What if he is so upset he never wants to speak to me again?

The response from one of my sons is probably the most loving thing he has ever done for me, further releasing me from my prison of abortion.

Dear Mom,
Thank you for being honest about this terrible thing...I know it must have been hard for you to share it with me, but honest, Mom, I hope you don't think I would hate you...I feel so sad for our family.
When I read your words, it was like all the puzzle pieces to my life fell into place. I don't know why, but I always felt like our family had a "missing piece"...Our home had an emptiness, an unexplainable sadness. Now I know why...
Thank you, Mom, for having the courage to share your heart. Now I know why you are so passionate about pro-life issues. Yes, it all makes sense now. I love you, Mom...

Taken from the January 2003 Focus on the Family magazine.
Copyright © 2003, Focus on the Family. Used by permission.

1.   **Do you sense that God is prompting you to tell a specific person about your abortion experience? Who is that person?**

2.   **How do you feel about the idea of disclosing your secret?**

DEAR YOUNGER SELF

Dear Younger Self,

I know how badly you would like to go back and do your life over. Perhaps you <u>truly believe</u> that it would be possible to make healthy choices instead of disastrous ones another time around. But do you know what? Even if you could do it all again, there would still be choices you would regret, because there is simply no such thing as a life lived without them. And those sad choices are what God has used to teach you about his endless love for you. If he didn't love you so much, how could he ever have asked his one and only Son to pay such a terrible price on your behalf?

Precious Younger Self, your pride and independence <u>had</u> to be broken one way or another. Can you now see that God <u>had</u> to allow you to experience the harsh consequences of sex outside of marriage, for your own good? That it wasn't until your soul was totally shattered that you finally cried out to him and allowed him to rescue and restore you? What do you suppose your life would be like if you <u>hadn't</u> undergone this complete remolding of your heart and soul? Probably pretty ghastly: stiff-necked pride and arrogant self-sufficiency are a very unpleasant combination.

I know that you resent the influences that caused you to behave as you did, to make the choices that you did. And I know you wish that you had had the faith, strength of character, and courage to face your crises and trust God in them. But the fact is that those choices have been made and there is no un-making them. All you can do is be deeply grateful that yours is a God who does the unthinkable: He has "swept away your sins like the morning mists and scattered your offences like the clouds." He begs you to "return to him for he has paid the price to set you free." Isaiah 44:32.

Now your challenge is to thank him by living as you should; to thank him by being an example of what it looks like to be a woman loved, redeemed, and restored by God; to thank him by leading others to the healing you have experienced; to thank him by sharing the joy of restoration; and to thank him by delighting in the fact that he calls you his most precious "Masterpiece!" Now, go in peace...

With love from,
Your Older, Wiser Self

Find a photo of your Younger Self at about the age your letter is addressing. Take some extra paper and write your own letter, by hand, to your Younger Self from your Older, Wiser Self. Tell her all that you now understand and all that you have learned.

HEALING JOURNEY CD

Sometimes certain songs describe our experiences in a way that we cannot.

Here is your opportunity to create a play list of eight tracks that speak of your recovery process. These songs may correspond with the chapters in your manual, or may simply refer to certain powerful experiences you have had over the course of the *Living in Color* program.

Use titles of actual songs or albums such as "Jagged Little Pill," "Who Will Stop The Rain," or "Amazing Grace." Alternatively, you may make up your own song titles. Choose a name for your CD and create a cover for it too, if you like.

1.   **Choose names for your eight songs and explain why you have chosen each name.**

PLAY LIST

Track One:

Track Two:

Track Three:

Track Four:

Track Five:

Track Six:

Track Seven:

Track Eight:

2.   **Now choose your album title and explain your choice.**

ALBUM TITLE

_____

3.   **Create your cover design on a separate piece of paper.**

Music is what feelings sound like.

Unknown

ALL OF ME

An experience that looms large in our lives may sometimes alter how we perceive ourselves. Just as some may define themselves as "divorced," "laid-off," or "disabled," an abortion experience can cause us to think of ourselves above all else as "post-abortive." Certain labels carry negative connotations that, if we are not careful, can smother all the other healthy and wonderful parts of who we are.

Now that you have experienced healing and restoration, it is time to reconnect with your wholeness: to reacquaint yourself with your unique, multi-faceted self.

1. **Sit and think about all the roles you play in your life. Jot them down as they come to mind, then fill up the pie below with as many as you can. Some ideas may be: friend, cyclist, neighbor, Christian, gardener, mentor, cook, nurse, coin collector, volunteer, book club member, fashionista, etc.**

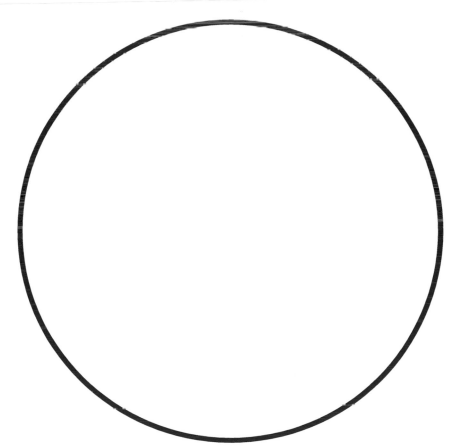

2. **How does it feel to see your whole self laid out before you? Take extra paper and use the following prompt to get started:**

    Contemplating all of who I am and naming all the roles I play in life makes me realize that...

FEELING GOOD ABOUT MYSELF

As we survey the weeks, months, or years since our abortions took place, many of us discover that we have developed habits that undermine our worth. These habits may prompt us to disrespect ourselves, neglect our health, or even take away our joy for living. For example, many years after healing, some women continue to withhold pleasurable experiences from themselves, simply out of habit.

This behavior has no place in our lives as whole, restored, healthy women. So, it's now time to focus on healthy living practices and to reconnect with our hopes and dreams.

1. **Jot down answers to the following as honestly as you can:**

    - **What do I like or value about myself?**

    - **How well do I care for my physical health?**

    - **How do I care for my emotional health?**

    - **How do I develop my spiritual journey?**

    - **What are my special gifts, talents, and skills?**

    - **How do I reward myself?**

    - **What are my hopes and dreams?**

    - **Am I living in the present?**

    - **What makes me laugh?**

- **When and how do I show affection?**

- **What makes me hopeful?**

- **How is my "Joy List" coming along?**

2. Imagine a good friend describing you to someone who is moving into the house next door to yours. Your new neighbor is looking forward to meeting you. Write a script of how your friend might describe the new person you are now.

GOD'S CALLING ON YOUR LIFE

Have you ever wondered what on earth you are supposed to do with your unique combination of personality, experiences, and giftedness? Here is a simple yet powerful exercise you can do to identify just what God's calling upon your life actually is. If your current work and/or activities seem more of a burden than a blessing, this process may be helpful for re-designing your future.

There are no "right" answers to these questions. In fact, understanding that everyone will have unique responses is essential. Try to be as spontaneous as possible for the first question and answer with just one word or short phrase.

If you need help with the second question, try thinking back to what made you feel most joyful and alive as a seven to ten-year-old child.

1.   **What is your perception of the world's greatest need?**

2.   **What is your greatest joy?**

3.   **Describe an experience that caused you to feel most joyful and fulfilled.**

4.   **Now carefully read this quote several times:**

God's calling on your life is to be found at the intersection of your perception of the world's greatest need and your greatest joy.

Frederick Buechner

5. Consider whether your life is in step with God's calling, as described in question four. Are you in that "sweet spot": responding to your perception of the world's greatest need *and* your greatest joy? Write a reflection on what your responses are revealing to you.

6. Write a prayer asking God to help you take ownership of all the gifts and talents you have to offer the world, and to help you discover ways to fulfill your potential.

Dear God,
   Thank you for creating me anew. Now, as I consider what to do with my life, I…

When you commit your dreams to paper
you give them a place to take root.

Terri Trespicio

CHOOSING JOY

Joy is what makes life worth living, but for many, joy seems hard to find...what then brings the joy we so much desire? Are some people just lucky, while others have run out of luck?

Strange as it may sound, we can choose joy. Two people can be part of the same event, but one may choose to live it quite differently from the other. One may choose to trust that what happened, painful as it may be, holds a promise. The other may choose despair and be destroyed by it.

What makes us human is precisely this freedom of choice.[12]

Henri Nouwen

1.   **You have already started to choose joy by creating your "Joy List." Add another couple of items to your list right now. Record them here as well.**

2.   **It's now time to bring your healing and recovery journey to a close. Focus on the joy that comes from choosing to believe that you are whole, worthy, beautiful, and deeply loved. Take time to select an item to bring to our closing session that represents the promise your future holds. Describe your item.**

3.   **Now finish by writing a reflection on why you have chosen this particular item. How does it symbolize the life you are choosing to live, beginning today?**

Whatever happens, dear sisters, may the Lord give you joy.

Philippians 3:1a

12   Henri Nouwen *Bread for the Journey* (New York: Harper Collins Publishers, 1997)

CONGRATULATIONS!

You can be justifiably proud of your achievement.

You have worked long and hard.

You have faced your loss and all its accompanying fallout.

You have told your story.

You have learned about the cost of denying your need to grieve.

You have gathered valuable understanding and tools for dealing with anger.

You have learned the importance of forgiveness and its power to change lives.

You have opened your heart to God who created you and your child.

You have allowed him to bring you healing and hope.

You have said "hello" to your child and have spent precious time together.

You have said "goodbye for now," knowing that your child awaits you in heaven.

You have learned how to grieve well.

You have been created anew by your courageous journey.

You have identified your unique gifts and talents.

You have learned to love and respect yourself.

And you are now poised to allow your wisdom, peace, faith, and joy
to mold your future.

May God bless you in all you do!

APPENDICES

APPENDIX A: HOW TO DO GROUP

Our journey together needs to be safe, compassionate, and effective. Here are a few tips for ensuring its success:

1. **Confidentiality**

   This is a closed group, which means the identity of group members and what is shared during group sessions is absolutely confidential. Please understand that disclosing any details outside of the group is a violation of trust. Each group member is asked to sign an Oath of Confidentiality to ensure the safety and security of everyone present.

2. **Homework**

   Each week your homework will involve reading, reflection, journaling, and writing answers to questions. Your written work is your preparation for the group sessions, and the more time, thought, and effort you put into your homework, the more healing you will achieve.

3. **Attendance**

   Regular attendance is usually not an issue. Everyone soon realizes that if she is not there, the others are healing without her! However, out of respect for the group, please arrive on time. We will do our best to finish our two-hour sessions promptly as well.

4. **Commitment**

   Even if you have to drag yourself to every session, do fight the temptation to quit the group. This is challenging work and your healing depends on completing the journey. However, if you do need to leave, please let your facilitators know.

5. **Flow**

   Everyone must feel welcome to speak, but do remember that others need a chance to share as well. At times, a great deal of pain will be expressed and many tears shed. Please don't attempt to stop the process by offering comfort, even though this may seem like a natural and compassionate reaction.

6. **Focus**

   An examination of your life may bring up other difficult issues, but this program's primary focus is on post-abortion healing. Keep a list of other issues as they arise; we will help you access suitable help once the program is finished.

7. **Materials**

   You may encounter all kinds of abortion materials on-line and in books, on TV, etc. Please check with your facilitators before exchanging any such materials (for the duration of the group).

8. **Support**

   If at all possible, try to find someone outside the group to support, encourage, and cheer you on as you complete this journey. If this person will pray for you too, so much the better.

APPENDIX B: CREATING A SANCTUARY

Grief work requires a place of solitude and few interruptions. This "sanctuary" may be a cozy window seat at home, a stretch of lawn outside, or even the front seat of your car if that is the only place you can be alone.

As you go to your sanctuary, you intentionally move from outer life to inner life. This deliberate transition is sometimes referred to as "structured grieving," and it allows you to manage your grief rather than being consumed by it.

You may find it helpful to place a few items such as a candle, some reminder of a baby or child, a single flower in a bud vase, your Bible, and a box of tissues in your sanctuary. And one of the most powerful tools of healing is a journal.

Once you have a place, you must set aside time to spend there each day. Ask yourself when you will feel most like moving inward to your homework. Then set aside time—perhaps just 15 minutes at first—and commit to completing at least a few segments each day. This will be far more effective than a mad scramble the night before the next group session. In a busy household you may have to get up early or stay up late to have quiet, uninterrupted time. Recognize that this sacrifice is temporary: do whatever it takes to create time to heal.

If you have time, or feel the need, journal writing over and above your homework will be very helpful. The more you write, the more you will process your grief. Try using the prompts on the following page to get you started. As you persist, you will break down the walls and begin to reach into the necessary places. Before long, your pen will race across the pages almost of its own accord.

As you make a practice of engaging with your inner life often, deeply, and honestly, you will gradually expose the "wounded places" to the air for cleansing and healing. Don't be surprised by the glimmers of hope that begin to emerge as healing takes place. Rather, highlight them as they appear in your writing.

Be prepared for the resistance you feel towards going to your sanctuary: you will find yourself thinking of dozens of other activities that seem far more urgent. This avoidance is your heart's way of trying to protect itself. But resisting will not get you through the pain or set you on the path to freedom. Just settle down and get to work—the reward will be well worth it!

1.   **Where will your sanctuary be?**

2.   **What will you place there to create a welcoming setting?**

3.   **When will you do your structured grieving?**

APPENDIX C: JOURNALING PROMPTS

- My upbringing led me to believe…
- My relationship with the father of my baby was…
- At the time I was emotionally…
- The overriding influence that caused me to choose abortion was…
- I can't believe that I…
- The lies I believed were…
- I convinced myself that…
- The risks I took included…
- I couldn't consider releasing for adoption because…
- I have tried to compensate by…
- I have punished myself by…
- Back then my thoughts about parenting were…
- At the time, my goals were…
- The most disappointing thing was…
- If only I had…
- What has surprised me most is…
- What made me push away was…
- Why didn't I…
- Why has it taken me so long to…
- Unhealthy strategies I have tried include…
- Coping with the fallout has…
- What I fear the most is…
- What I have learned about myself is…
- What I long for is…
- The thing that made me seek help was…
- What I look forward to the most is…

APPENDIX D: WHAT'S YOUR FAVORITE SENSE?

Choose only one answer from each question, and circle the letter next to your answer.

1. If only three rooms are left at a beach resort, I'll choose the room that offers
    (a) an ocean view but lots of noise
    (b) sounds of the ocean but no view
    (c) comfort but lots of noise and no view

2. When I have a problem
    (a) I look for alternatives
    (b) I talk about the problem
    (c) I rearrange the details

3. When riding in a car, I want the inside to
    (a) look good
    (b) sound quiet and powerful
    (c) feel comfortable and secure

4. When I explain a concert or event I've just attended, I first
    (a) describe how it looked
    (b) tell people how it sounded
    (c) convey the feeling

5. In my spare time, I most enjoy
    (a) watching TV or going to the movies
    (b) reading or listening to music
    (c) doing something physical (craft/gardening) or playing a sport

6. The one thing I personally believe everyone should experience in their lifetime is
    (a) sight
    (b) sound
    (c) feeling

7. Of the following activities, I spend the most time indulging in
    (a) daydreaming
    (b) listening to my thoughts
    (c) picking up on my feelings

8. When someone is trying to convince me of something
    (a) I want to see evidence or proof
    (b) I talk myself through it
    (c) I trust my intuition

185

9. I usually speak and think
    (a) quickly
    (b) moderately
    (c) slowly

10. I normally breathe from
    (a) high in my chest
    (b) low in my chest
    (c) my belly

11. When finding my way around an unfamiliar city,
    (a) I use a map
    (b) I ask for directions
    (c) I trust my intuition

12. When I choose clothes, it is most important to me that
    (a) I look immaculate
    (b) I make a personal statement
    (c) I feel comfortable

13. When I choose a restaurant, my main concern is that
    (a) it look impressive
    (b) I can hear myself talk
    (c) I will be comfortable

14. I make decisions
    (a) quickly
    (b) moderately
    (c) slowly

Excerpted from *How to Make People Like You in 90 Seconds or Less*
Copyright 2000, 2008 by Nicholas Boothman
Used by permission of Workman Publishing Co., Inc., New York
All Rights Reserved

APPENDIX E: WHAT'S YOUR FAVORITE SENSE? ANALYSIS

Add up and record the number of times you have circled each letter in the WHAT'S YOUR FAVORITE SENSE questionnaire:

(a) _____ A majority of "a" responses means that you are **VISUAL**

(b) _____ A majority of "b" responses means that you are **AUDITORY**

(c) _____ A majority of "c" responses means that you are **KINESTHETIC**

The higher the number is in each category, the stronger the tendency is at work in your life. This may help you to select your preferred sense when you have a choice. For example: When asking for directions, a visual person will find a map or sketch more helpful than spoken instructions.

You will also understand why people engage with the world in such different ways, and make allowances accordingly. And you can choose the most natural method for your grief work—writing, talking, massage, walking, sketching, collage, or listening to music—as appropriate.

1. **My favorite sense is:**

2. **How do you feel about your results? Is this information a surprise to you? Does it explain why you respond to things differently from your family or friends?**

3. **Can you see, hear, or sense, that knowing this about yourself may be helpful in many areas of your life?**

APPENDIX F: GRIEVING SUMMARY

Grieving can be bewildering, especially since most people are not taught how to handle grief well. There are numerous different ways to grieve, many of which you have experienced throughout this *LIVING IN COLOR* program.

These reminders may be helpful in the future:

- Allow yourself to think deeply about what or whom you have lost
- Feel the pain
- Cry, cry, cry
- Soak in the bath and let your thoughts and emotions roam
- Physically let go of something that represents a part of the grief process
- Take a contemplative walk
- Engage in strenuous activity to release physical tension
- Perform a healing ritual
- Join a support group
- Get counseling help
- Talk, talk, talk
- Embrace the support of those who care
- Look for supportive scriptures in the Bible
- Express and release emotions through journaling
- Write—but do not send—anger and forgiveness letters
- Write poetry or compose music
- Create: quilt, paint, garden, embroider, make collages, etc.
- Listen to music that expresses your pain or soothes your soul
- Light candles
- Hold a memorial service
- Engage constructively with anniversaries
- Establish a foundation
- Make a donation of time or money to a meaningful cause
- Create a memorial
- Send yourself flowers

RESOURCES

ORDERING INFORMATION:

LIVING IN COLOR: THE GOAL OF POST-ABORTION RECOVERY
www.createspace.com/3464277

LIVING IN COLOR FACILITATOR GUIDE:
www.pregcare.com
info@pregcare.com

FOR RECOVERY HELP FOLLOWING ABORTION, PLEASE CONTACT:

www.pregcare.com
info@pregcare.com

RECOMMENDED READING:

FAMILY TIES THAT BIND: A SELF-HELP GUIDE TO CHANGE THROUGH FAMILY OF ORIGIN THERAPY
By Dr Ronald W. Richardson
ISBN 1-55180-238-4

WHERE TO DRAW THE LINE: HOW TO SET HEALTHY BOUNDARIES EVERY DAY
By Anne Katherine
ISBN 0-684-86806-7

WOMEN AND SADNESS: A SANE APPROACH TO DEPRESSION
By M. Sara Rosenthal
ISBN 978-0771576294